# *Reflections and Emotions*

To Mick & Fran
Special friends
Frances
9/29/10

# Reflections and Emotions

## Frances H. Kunzweiler

iUniverse, Inc.
New York   Bloomington

# REFLECTIONS AND EMOTIONS

iUniverse books may be ordered through booksellers or by contacting:

iUniverse
1663 Liberty Drive
Bloomington, IN 47403
www.iuniverse.com
1-800-Authors (1-800-288-4677)

ISBN: 978-1-4502-2168-9 (pbk)
ISBN: 978-1-4502-1568-8 (ebook)

Printed in the United States of America

iUniverse rev. date: 5/24/10

# Contents

# FOREWORD

*This my third book reveals additional introspective ,thoughts and feelings about my life, faith, family, friends, our country, the economy and more. The previous two publications, My Musings and Me, and Memories and Musings brought to fruition a life-long dream.*

*I am grateful for the blessings of longevity, good health, a loving family, countless friends and sincere belief in the power of prayer. Having experienced life's challenges, disappointments, joys and successes during my 95 years I tried to meet each a certain kind of God given optimism.*

*For those who peruse these pages, I encourage positive thinking and hope about the future. The scientific milestones achieved and incredible advances in medicine, invention and electronic wizardry during my lifetime are almost incomprehensible. Somehow we have to believe there can be peace among nations of the world, and an end to suffering and strife.*

*One just has to wonder what the next 95 years will bring.*

*This book, as the previous two is dedicated to my late husband Joe, my son Don, my daughter Rita and my grandchildren Karen, Rick, Tim, Denny, Tricia; my great grandchildren Chelsea, Callahan, Joe, Stephanie; and great-great grandchildren Chase and Maddison. They are forever in my thoughts and prayers.*

*To everyone who reads this volume, may you be abundantly blessed in every way. Life is good!*

*Frances Helen Kunzweiler*

# PICTURE FRAME

While looking in the attic among things of yesteryears
Memories came back to haunt me bringing many smiles and tears
Remembering good times we enjoyed, our lives not known for fame
I found something to always cherish pictured in an antique frame.

Hanging in a dusty corner where no one seemed to care
Was this heirloom so beautiful with a couple seated there
Standing silent for a minute, hands trembling, head bent low
Seems to me you were whispering, "As years pass our love will grow."
The frame I dusted gently, oh to live those years again
Still that love has never faded neither has the antique frame...

# *A LOVE LETTER**

To his darling in the morning:

My dearest come back again, my heart is broken my darling
This absence and silence ceases
Send me a message, twill soften my anguish
And wake up the sweet fervor so blest of yore with passion.
Sparkling gray eyes that beameth in me
Tempting ripe lips – oh how soon you forget
How my heart in its loving devotion
Its idol is the master to all thee met.

Come back my loving one I pine and I languish
To see thee again
Where happiness are over my spirit
Long memories are thronging
Send me they post napp and list to my prayer
Roses in the morning
Make the day so bright
Thrilling every corner
With a gleam of light
And what happiness she misses
Who departs and gave no kisses
To his darling in the morning.

*written by my Grandfather John Edwards
to his beloved Ruth in the late 1800s.

# GRANDFATHER JOHN EDWARDS

Late in the year 1875, he sailed back to England, the country
Of his birth, from New York on the steamship City of Chester.
While there he met a young lady twenty-three years of age. He
Wooed and won her affection though her parents were most
Unhappy about the situation as John was so much older.
After a whirlwind courtship, John won the parents consent to marry
Ruth Sharpe who had been a lady in waiting to a royal princess.
Following their marriage in Liverpool, England they sailed to
America on the steamship "Germania" arriving in New York
On January 19, 1876.

# GRANDMOTHER RUTH SHARPE

Born in Emberton, Buckingham, suburb of London,
At age twenty-three she met John Edwards at a party.
They were married in Liverpool and shortly thereafter
Sailed to the America on the steamship Germania.
Following the long journey, arrived in New York
Thence settling in rural Illinois.
Bearing eight children, five sons, three daughters,
My grandfather died in 1887, while Grandma Ruth lived to be
99 years old. She was a grand lady who loved life
And I remember her from visits
A life she lived
One to give
Born on English sod
Loving to dance
Now in remembrance
She lives in the grace of God.

# HERE'S TO THE HEROES

Here's to the heroes so gallantly brave
Volusia and Flagler they united to save
Firemen, police, volunteers, doctors and nurses
Houligan's, Daytona 500 opened their purses.

Clergy, churches, businesses, the National Guard too—
Donations poured in from me and from you
Newspapers, TV, radio gave up their time
Telephone workers kept us on-line.

Tired and weary with mercy and might
Not one firefighter gave up the perilous fight
From states represented all will acclaim,
"The worst ever seen" was this inferno of flame.

Now drive along highways, forest is bare
We've so many to thank (and God did his share)
There will be memories, laughter and mirth
And tales of fires that ravished our earth.

By Frances Helen Kunzweiler

*Written in tribute and included in*
*A Book of Poems*
*Commemorating*
*WILDFIRE Florida 1998*
*A hundred year event*
*IBSN: 07392-0066-6*
*Library of Congress Catalog Card Number 998-94925*

# WORK OF ART

To the greater glory of God

Many lonely hours I've spent
Since we have been apart
Sands of time leave etchings
Like a noble work of art

Look up at the vastness
A plane streaks cross the sky
Know without the hand of God
Not even birds could fly.

After storms watch the rainbow
Water glistening on the land
Thirsty earth was gladdened
The struggling farmer clasps his hand.

Long days pass more quickly
Listen, I will tell you why
The day of partying gone forever
A work of art, the butterfly.

Flits around from flower to flower
Adding beauty to the land
Birds in radiant color
Captured by the artist's hand.

Learn of glory everywhere
Etchings are a part
The chance to be living
Enjoying the Master's work of art.

# TENDER THOUGHTS

I was going to write a sonnet
One morning about the dew
There was a rabbit in the garden
In Florida we see very few
Made me stop and wonder
Was a child's pet on the loose?
It did not seem a stranger
Hopped around looking hungry
Spied a lovely patch of clover
Quickly mowed it to a mound
Then at nightfall the wondrous
Deer silently arrive
Quickly but still, no sound
On hibiscus plants they thrive
A blossom first, leaves next
Then tender shoots, sakes alive
Leaving nothing, but sticks abound
Often a reminder of their visit
Is found on the ground.

+ + +

# A PERSONAL NOTE!

*THE 20TH DAY*

*THE MONTH*

*JULY*

*THE YEAR*

*2009*

*IT'S GREAT*

*BEING ALIVE*

*REACHING*

*AGE 95*

# LIFE

A mirage of highways
Many bridges crossed
Angels search skyways
Looking for the lost
Humanity living this world over
Near and far apart
Soon enjoy prosperity
With love and prayer a start
Enjoy life
A new beginning
All lend a hand
Be charitable
Provide opportunities
Be empathetic and understanding
Sing "God Bless America"
All who realize their freedom
Here on planet earth
Land of their birth.


Pain and Fear
Might cause a tear
Listen to laughter
Tis joy you're after
Soon to smile again
Give a sigh
When the sun is high
Sing a happy refrain.

.

# *LOVE*

A touch of hope will follow
As you pass by
Wander a path of love
Tell me you will try
Make the most of memories
Along life's way
Few lines will help overcome
Unhappiness I pray
There is someone watching
On a distant shore
Fill your heart, be a part
One who wanders no more.

# *AMEN*

You will never be alone my friend
At the end of a prayer, whisper Amen.

# *SEAL*

Live with intention
Be sure to mention
Happy you are today
Share time with others
Your guardian angel leads the way
Gossip I hear
Isn't meant for my ear
Not interested what they say or saw
Many have a flaw
Plain old me living my way
Cannot change life
How I feel – just write a few lines each day
Wishing sometimes
My ears to seal.

# FAITH

With faith we gain knowledge
Leads us to understand
We reach out tomorrow
God is there with helping hand
Really not an effort
Praying each day
We might travel longer
And blessings fill the way.

# SHE CARES

Blessed mother mine
Prayer is offered for all mankind
Simple understanding
Let not our faith be lost
Reaching your destination
No penny will it cost.

# CHASE

Having on a pair of shoes
Great great-grandson Chase age 6
"Grandma, those are really neat"
Telling him they were *Grasshoppers*
Yelling for his mother
Mom come quick
Grandma's wearing
Grasshoppers on her feet.

# FUN

May hearts be full of love
Minds with dedication
A few moments daily
A valued education
Sharing good deeds
Travel roads with happiness
Treasure what you find
Friends needed by everyone
Keep your mind occupied
Pretend a 5K run
Life is filled with fun.

# RECOLLECTIONS

Having traveled through mountains
Stop to rest miles high
Scenes will enthrall you
Seems where earth meets the sky
Wander down the other side
Did it really seem
Close your eyes
Say to yourself
Am I living in a dream?
Water flowing majestically
Rippling far below
Take pictures wondrous earth
Created thousands of years ago.

# MY MOTHER LOTTIE

Mother's day 2008
Remember the joy of mine
I celebrate
My mom was born in 1890
That was long ago
Life wasn't easy back then.

I am one of eight
Youngest of three girls
Five boys followed
Some always on the go
I still write and wonder why
Event full days just happen
Helping out when I can.

Thinking back,
I loved my mom and dad
Things were different
Kids never did talk back
My sisters and I
Took care of my five brothers
Taught them how to write, read, act
Remembering all
When Mother's Day comes around
All gone to the great beyond

# PETALS

Petals from my memory book
Pressed between the pages
From a rose of long ago
Seemed thoughts of years
Brought about tears
I let them overflow.

Something that shows in a garden
Can also be found on a hill
A gift for all even strangers
Known to each God's will.

Reach out when there are problems
Why waste another day
Ask for help, you will find
Nothing stands in the way.

Life, love, laughter, happiness
May be found in a very small space
Pick a few petals for living
From the bouquet filled with grace.

Never turn from forgiveness
Though pain, wear smiles on your face
Come on mankind remember
We run the human race.

What if colors are different
Life's ambition we hope to fill
Stand straight and tall as the willow
Drink from the fountain of good will

# *HOPE*

Faith a stranger to many
Hope a promise to all
May each be blessed for knowledge
A gift I often recall.

# *SKILL*

The snow lays heavy on the ground
Cold winds give me a chill
If wondering why all this must be
The Master's shown his skill.
He shrouds each branch with beauty rare
Shines the sun in glory
Glistening icicles are everywhere
Like a fairy tale story.
As a child I walked to school
On snow above fence tops high
With no modern conveniences
Still we managed to get by
I guess I'm still a kid at heart
'cause when the winter comes
I hope it snows to fill the earth
So please don't feel glum
No artist does what God can do,
The skill that He can show
He makes the rain and rivers
And trees that grow and grow
I love every earthly thing
And people who live in it
No one could do a better job
But I can write a sonnet.

# TICK TOCK

A heartbeat tiny
Like ticking of a clock
No one can live without it
People say be still my heart
Many times stress, worry comes alive
Tis then pain expresses
Takes, gives time to reply
Doctors say to me, live easy
Use care in what you plan
Remember good health
Is vital for each human.

# OH!

Driving down the highway
Sign reads "Slow down, don't pass
Petrol next station
Is out of gas."

# ENTITLED

Love of people
Wonderful
Guard it night and day
If you travel a proper road
You have won the right of way.

# DOUBT

Smiling when happy
Show life is worthwhile
When one you know is lonely
Offer them a smile
They grasp it most eagerly
Do you have a plan?
Enlisted as a young man
He said, I'm going off to war
Mom never understood
What we were fighting for
Claiming youth from many
In our neighborhood
Knowing, hoping, praying
Serving for the common good.

# CARE LESS

Sending more troops to fight
They have only one life to live
Do you suppose it possible
How much must we forgive?
Wake up America
You can sing or shout
We have suffered enough.

No more orders from Washington
Wasting billions needlessly
From the start
Did any of them lend a hand
Not caring what was spent
"Stay the Course" *his* remark
His cost, not one cent.

# PHONES

Sitting in quiet comfort
Telephone rings give a summer alert
Stop day dreaming, answer quickly
Someone may be hurt.

Are there phones in heaven
Like people everywhere
Homes, schools, driving cars
If angels use them daily
Whom do they call for repair?

Electronics a need for everyone
Remote controls for everything
Seems like automation
Has a grip on the nation
Even used on television
Putting gasoline in your car
Costs four dollars per gallon
Install push buttons everywhere you please
Take time to relax
Why not have a button
To erase your income tax.

# THROUGH THE YEARS

Thank you good people
Living on Foxfords Chase
Now thirteen years have passed
Since we moved to Florida
To our home at Number Ten.

The warmer weather I enjoy most
Come visit any time
Our mat glows "welcome"
Let us enjoy being your host.

# QUIP

When things you are told
Not meant to flip
Be very cautions
Your tongue does not slip.

Do not lie on Sunday morning
Get up, go to church

# LIFE GOES ON

Be a dreamer
An ordinary plan
Walk a highway
Fly the skyway
Reach out, when you can.

Many feel neglected
Yet many coming home
From Iraq or Afghanistan
Say they are forgotten
No work, no joy, no life
Who the hell gives a "damn?"

Called to serve their country
For people in great need
Now you ask why
But get no reply
Was it to satisfy *someone's* greed?

Now for our troops
We must say a prayer
God bless and keep them
I believe they dream
Their path leads somewhere.

# OCTOBER TWELFTH

October brings a cooler breeze
Sunny skies above
Birds of paradise abloom
Ti plants red as scarlet
Greet a beautiful full moon
Rita celebrates her birthday
October 12
She is going to Nevada
Where Las Vegas dwells
Enjoys playing the slots
Hoping for a jackpot
That would be swell
My wish for her when going
I hope you win a lot
You may have a better time
Putting quarters, not dollars
In the slot.

# SPRING

Sun is shining
Flowers blooming
Thunder, lightning
We are assuming
Rain start falling
For a thirsty lawn
Leaving small puddles
For mama deer and fawn
Soon everything
Beautiful and green
Trees showing leaves
Sure enough tis spring
Stroll around pool deck
Should I get busy
Start cleaning
Maybe let me check
Decided, jump in the pool
Tomorrow will do
Today, what the heck.

# THINK

Time flies like an arrow.

Fruit flies like a banana!

## YOU PAY

Days pass quickly
When an idea comes your way
Soon the phone is ringing
May I visit you today
We could stop for a burger and coke
I'll pick you up if you will pay
That would be so nice you see
Because I am nearly broke.

## OH WELL

Did you know King Arthur's table
Was *Sir Cumference!*

## NIX

Trying to write with a pencil
With no idea why
It would not write
Because it was pointless.

# PERSONALITY

A great life given me
Mind to think, eyes to see
Ears to hear when you speak
Mouth accepted to answer back
If in pain being helpful
Memories gain
Legs to walk, toe nails to cut
Don't forget arms and fingers
Use your mind
Good thoughts linger

# TIME

Years I ponder when busy
Oft times I wonder
Stupidly doing things
Make me dizzy
Many things happening
Songs of the ages
Yellow the pages.

# *DUBAI*

The years spent in Chatham
Neighbors were great
All were of the best
Many had children
One in particular, Stacey VanderHeiden.

She grew-up next door on Crestview Drive
After college married Izzet
Now the family and lives in Dubai
With 3 sons, Benjamin, Nathaniel and Zachary
She and Izzet welcome baby girl Rachel Helen
A beautiful sister for the boys
Arrived in San Antonio, Texas state
On 4 August 2008
The happy occasion was greeted by
Grandpa and grandma Bob & Peg
Who motored there not to be late.

# *2007*

The year 2007
Many things happen
In our home now twelve years
Having moved from the freezing, ice and snow
Dreary winters of Illinois
We love Florida living
Ormond Beach is a real peach.
Time to have the house painted
And a new brick driveway installed
Making the home all new again
Our cup is full to the brim.
The neighbors all say, oh boy
Offering compliments of joy
Like a child with a new toy.
A man's home is his castle
Home is where the heart is
Old clichés state
And how very true
For us is ours
At 10 Foxfords Chase.

# *CURIOUS*

Did you hear about

The person stealing a calendar

Getting a year plus twelve months!

# FRIENDS

A day time of happiness
A memory to hold dear
Meeting at "Howie in the Hills"
Filled with friends for many years

Crowley and Markus
Mike & Sharon and Steve & Marilyn
Met there for lunch one day
Then stopped at the great little bakery
Bought goodies to share
Starting for home
Goodbyes were difficult to say
A wave of the hand
A goodbye kiss blown
All said, we must do this again
When next time we roam.

# WHO CARES

Where did you go Year 2007
Those who died by the thousands
Were welcomed into heaven
Martyrs in the Iraq fiasco
War ravished countries
Continuing
What the belief
For a hideous cause
Days of repentance
Another year fighting
Not even worth time mentioning.

# IF AND WHEN

Do you suppose
The Bush years
Will leave memories
Worthy of print
Articles in a national library?

# DUMB ME

Good man neighbor Bob VanderHeiden
Lived next door to me
Did me a great favor
How dumb could I be
Bob could fix anything
When something went wrong
His repair of clocks
No one missed his care
I purchased a small clock
Located in a dome
The salesman said
I don't think it runs
Try it when you get home
Took it to Bob next door
In ten minutes he returned laughing
To relate
I fixed it!
All it needed
Only a battery
To operate.

# *2008*

A new year 2008
Seems I make mistakes
Over and over
'Til my heart aches
Using a walker
At times a push chair
Enjoy going places
When weather is fair
Trying to write
For me a pleasure
Second book published
Sending to friends
And families to treasure.

# *QUIPS*

*When the fog lifts in Los Angeles*
*U.C.L.A.*

*The 2 tired bicycle*
*Cannot stand alone.*

*Did you hear about*
*The dentist and manicurist*
*Fighting tooth and nail.*

*Leaving a will*
*A dead gift.*

# *MARILYN*

Holding a baby in my arms
She was ten days old
They named her Marilyn Joan
Mom Emma and dad Mike
Brother Robert sister Eleanor Jean
They said she's too small
For us to hold
Grandma Barbara Groesch
Looked at Marilyn saying
She was a winner.
Oft times I could baby sit
When mom and dad went to dinner
The best time of all
She was three years old
A little red wagon
Her dad brought home
I could take her for a stroll.

# QUESTIONED

Recently asked by a friend
What do you think about
The one man's war
What in the world
Is the USA fighting for?

Thousands lives lost
Billions spent
Sorrow for suffering
Not worth a cent.

Being told it will last
Six months at most
"Mission accomplished"
Then send more troops
Ammunition, equipment, planes
Ignore injury, death and cost.

Pray people in all countries
Far and near
Soon the end of
"One man's war"

More than four thousand
I pray all went to heaven
At peace in a place
All sins forgiven.

# *PEACE*

March 17 – St. Pat's Day
Wearing the green
Enjoying every season
Many so far in 2008
Have small chance to redeem
Payments here, there, everywhere
Cost growing higher
Many homes, locations
No money means no buyer
Each one's home
Their own mansion
Regardless the size
Our country large
We all live in
Enjoy, love, family, neighbors
Gives each unknown pleasure
Education, help when needed
Knowledge, imagination
Like brilliant stars and moon
One item seems forgotten
Leaders who accommodate
So no war was needed
The world might celebrate.

# PRAY

Sending more troops
From a great freedom nation
Money being spent
Ravishing all creation
Businesses closing
Jobs by thousands lost
Housing country wide
Not worth its cost
Soldiers in hospitals
Like Washington's Walter Reed
Seems officials do not really care
Or see their desperate need.

May the injured be blessed
Given tender care
Toward full recovery
Knowing we keep them in prayer.

# FUN

2008 started with fun
Around the house
Because the cat
Caught the mouse.

May each day bring joy
Running *up* the *down* hall.

# BACK HOME IN CHATHAM

Who in the world may still remember
What we all did to enjoy Crestview Drive
In the village of Chatham, Illinois
Christmas trees, decorations most beautiful
Homes adorned
Neighbors, greetings extended
One great time, memory relived
When Garland Crouch came home
His helicopter landed
In the cul de sac
In front of our home
An exciting event.
Hoot Gibson faithfully
Used his snow plow to clean the driveways
What a kind neighborly thing to do.
Bob VanderHeiden fixed clocks
Herschel Cudworth, the master of many things
Grew fruit and veggies great to eat
Generously provided us many a treat
Steve and Marilyn Markus
Always volunteers for Air Rendezvous show
Best down to earth people
Anyone could know.
Mike and Sharon Crowley
Great they are, always will be
Wish soon they visit again
To Florida, Don and me.

# *THINKING*

One Cent

Think about this little joke
Keep a penny in your pocket
And never be broke.


When

I kept cool at a baseball game
Standing next to a fan.


Gas

Best way to save
If you want to travel far
Buy yourself a Harley
Get rid of your car.


Why did the football coach
Go to the bank
Because he wanted to get
His quarterback.

# WAYS

Trains on the track
Klickity clack
When rolling down the rails

Planes in the sky above
Leave long white contrails

Passengers hope to arrive on time
Appointments to fulfill

Cars on Interstate 95
Across the United Sates
Pray they are cautious
And no problems to relate

Cars, bikes, horses, dogs, boats
Race here in Daytona Beach
All have their favorites to win
Applause when the goal within reach.

# ONE WORD...

Therein is only one word
In the English language
From which ten words can be made
Without rearranging them.

He

Ere

In

Her

Here

Herein

The

There

Rein

Therein

*Just a bit of trivia!*

# THE GUNEYS

Blessings Stacey and Izzet "Ike"
For the new baby
I am elated over Rachel Helen
For brothers Ben, Zack and Nathaniel.

Given over ninety years ago
My first name is Helen
Back then everyone said
An English name to know
I will feel like a great grandma
Not any relation though
With Stacey growing up next door.

To me a companion
Worth more than imagination
Bob and peg her parents
Proud as they could be
Never causing problems
A beautiful Miss Stacey
Was great company for me.

Especially when Don would travel
She would visit many times
Our thoughts would unravel
Those days in Chatham, Illinois
Our swimming pool brought many joy.

# *2007*

I will remember 2007
My dream came true
Started at age eleven
Writing poetry but having no clue
My works to be published
Two books beautifully accomplished
By "*IUniverse*"

The first entitled "*My Musings and Me*"
Next "*Musings and Memories*"
Original art work by Sr. Pauletta Overbeck
Lovely white and pink covers
Printing sublime
Read both discover
Much enjoyment you find.

# MIRTH

Snow on mountains
Lasts periods of time
Feeling of contentment
Fill heart and mind
Enjoy each moment
Full of mirth
No expense for mother earth.

# SHADOWS

The highway of life
We all travel
At times seem paved with stone
Sunshine casts a shadow
You talk out loud
Suddenly you realize
You are alone by imagination
Beginning to feel proud
Memories begin to haunt you
Shining sun brightens your day
Starting with doubt
You begin to shout
My life started over today.

# M AND M

May musings bring happiness
Memories recall
Time in your life
Treasures for all
Lighten your mind
Put a smile on your face
The sun will shine
Frowns erase
Shake away anger
Laugh as you will
Pleasure no cost
Your cup to fulfill.

# MOON

The sun will shine
Moon aglow
Stars everywhere
A magnificent overflow
Items like these
Impossible to buy
Belonging to heaven
High in the sky.

# BUILD

Bless those who pray
Help those who stray
Like man creates a frame
Use talent, ideas
Mold an image
They give all a name
Doing something useful
Plans will delight
Happiness follows
Make mistake
Let wrong turn out right.

# IRISH CREAM

Enjoy a holiday
Visit in Ireland
View man with team
Singing when tilling land
We enjoyed our bus ride
Traveling everyday
Stopped for a sip of Irish coffee
Then continued on our way.

# *REALLY*

The harder I try, behinder I get
From morn to set of sun
An answer to these I believe and told
The older one gets, the slower you run.

# FOLKS SAY

Folks say what are you doing
Ask questions by the dozen
Who are you writing about
Aunts, nieces, cousins

One said, I'm not good with words
Another, I do not cook
We eat at restaurants
Most of the time
Wondering how to answer
Enough is enough
Sharing ideas
Not my antidote
To me tis like
Shaking powder from a puff.

# LONG AGO

Way back in the 40's
Down on the farm
Trees were cut down
Limbs in small pieces
Kindling used for keeping
Home and families warm.

Summer came
We had an orchard
Grape vines, veggies
Grown in long rows.

Harvest time in the Fall
Filling the cellar to overflow
Educated in a one room school
Very little trouble
Was the Golden Rule.

Holidays we enjoyed
Thanksgiving and Christmas
Days were fine
Those days gave the teacher
A chance to unwind.

# TRIVIA

Q. When someone asks me
Where will you find
The deepest part of the ocean
A. At the bottom dummy.


Q. What do people use
for fishing from ships?
A. North and south poles.

# THANKS

Mick and Fran Ryan
Enjoy my books of poetry
Sent a thank you to me
You Irish are the greatest
A happy loving couple
Living life cheerfully.

# NO WANNABE

Saying you're brilliant
Casts a shadow today
Training to be kind
Assisting any way
Is a kind deed many say.

"I wannabe"
How does this apply
To accept life, your job
Education, family especially
Friends never allow jealousy
To enter their mind.

With all the stresses of today
Bankruptcies, jobs lost, foreclosures
Maybe offer of a friendly hand
Will help in a small way.

A sunny day put care away
Grasp them by the hand
We still live, forget, forgive
The U.S. still our promised land.

# A THOUGHT

Wandering away on a bright sunny day
Viewing ways of life
Seeing suffering humanity in a struggle
Of life's devastation
Greeting each year with hope
After happening of 9/11
Thousands lost, billions cost
Will those responsible be forgiven?

# AGAIN

Don is landscaping
Using sod, mulch, rock, stone
Many times and many days
No help, all alone
Takes hours of planning
Yet when trees, shrubs bloom
A hot sunny day
We hope storms stray
Bring no hurricanes no gloom.

# HOPE

I know there is heaven
Purgatory and place called hell
Your plan should be
Where the angels dwell.

During life's span take a stand
Pray for the best
We're all God's children
Someday each hope
Being best an invited guest.

# ONE

One life to life
One to give
Doing a good deed
Learning, gaining knowledge
Start with hope, succeed
The intellectual person
Will reap a harvest
From each planted seed.

# RECALL

What is memory
Something happened when a child
Might last a lifetime
Make years worthwhile
Preteen years together
Loving parents smile
Going on vacations together
Those times passed quickly
High school four years
Soon passed by
College on the horizon
One you have chosen
Keep your memory book
Teen years you loved them all
Many you knew departed
Time spent pleasure bent recall
Graduation, dances, parties
Take teen years grown-ups
Back to where they started.

# *ANOTHER YEAR*

Strange ways, troubled days
Tomorrow may bring
Let all enjoy a morning
With a tremendous spring.

Summer time explodes
With  temperatures in the 90s
A sure thing.
Put on swim suits
Use oil protect skin secure
Next back to school in August
A time to be demure.

No delay for the hurricanes
Time will pass rapidly
Halloween, Thanksgiving
Holidays to celebrate
Then comes December soon
Christmas on the way.

Sleigh bells ring bring happiness of yesterday
Oh too soon it seems
Twenty-o-nine is gone
But new year twenty-ten
A whole new one to stay.

# JERRY SCOTT

Jerry Scott a nephew kind generous man
Did everything he could
During his life's span
His dad Ray, mom Louise, my sister
Lived next door to me
Younger than my son Don
And daughter Rita
Both boys liked to tease.
Jerry had a small red wagon
A bulldog named Junior
He would hitch him to the wagon
Ride all around the neighborhood
Even in a downtown parade
Real, no charade.

Suddenly grown to a handsome young man
Married Margaret "Peggy" Scott
A career in Navy submarine service
Once anchored in Hawaii
He took me and his mom below
Something I never forgot
Now Jerry is in heaven
Taken from all too soon
His legacy lives on
To me and a loving family
His life meant a lot.

# WORLD

Fires in California
Floods from Midwest
Thousands left homeless
Folks losing homes a mess
Business closings
Schools, banks churches
Each day something more
Many people wonder
What caused all this to ponder.

The war, unnecessary
Costing ten billion each month
While people in our country suffer
Prices of gas, grocery and everyday living
Cars not selling, economy stalling
Airlines quitting service
Conditions making everyone nervous.

Still we must have faith and remember
There is God
Who created all humanity
Watching ever patiently
Trust in Him and pray
Situations will improve each day.

# REFLECTING

Living in the country
Many years ago
From top of hill to lower ground
You would holler
Hello-hello
Echoes came back
When we said
"You're walking slow"
One time someone answered
We are here,
It's you who's down below.

Things we did for entertainment
Back then climb
From valley to top of hill
Reminders of yesterday
Better than a good health pill.

Today at 94 years of age
Enjoy going other places
Yet in memory not forget
A life of pleasure lived
Seen many changes,
Written many pages.

# *HISTORY*

Never climbed the Matterhorn
Or wanted to be an astronaut
But flew planes many times
Like the one called Ozark
No queue lines needed
Nor endless waiting time.

Coke way back then
Cost a shiny dime
Tip was a half-a-dollar
Now in 2008,
Not sure of the price
Airport check-in no longer nice
Examine bags, purses, pockets, even shoes
Lengthy waits for security
Whatever happened to maturity
Planes today fly faster
Airline travel costs an arm and a leg
Used to be lots of amenities
Free movies, drinks and food
Now we pay for everything good.

Now me at 93
Thinking back at what used to be
In 30's and 40's, gas 24 cents a gallon
Driving coast to coast
Cost us $25 we'd boast.
Movies were ten cents
Balcony seating, the most.
Oh well, guess I'll now relax
Go travel in my Cadillac
Fill the tank for 60 bucks
Go to the store and back.

# MAYBE

Being great-great grandma
Great 5th generation
Makes me wonder many times
About our foreign nations
How people live, doing for others
In serious situations.

Employment limited leaves many in doubt
Entire world suffering
As everyone's problems mount.
Wondering if a future
For young students everywhere
A need for prayer to the creator
Will keep us in His care.

# NO USE

I would plant a garden
For eating to delight
However deer, rabbits and armadillos
Eat them before they are ripe.

# *PEGGY*

Loving days of memory
Happy times we shared
After glowing echoing
From someone who cared
Laughing days many ways
Recalling funny times
Leaving pain, grief behind
Be a dreamer when you can
Arise to the sunny sky
Make someone's burden lighter
Think of your family's love
David, Mike, Randy, Toyi
Happiness antidotes
Blue skies up above
My memories include
Hawaii was really great
Having a trip oh boy
On the anchored submarine
When our dresses flew
Blew over our heads
Showing a lot of leg
Gosh did those guys enjoy.

# OH MY

Looking for winter coat
Not wool nor leather
Clerk came back
One in hand
Saying try this on
Left over from spring
Lighter than a feather.

# WONDER

Anyone have a question
Curious I ask
When are you going out again
Where to, what is your path
We don't know til moving
There will be lots of water
One yelled and enough to take a bath

# POETRY IS EXCITING

Poetry is exciting
Written for people you know
If not by the hundreds
The author lets happiness overflow.
Mom, dad, sisters, brothers
Not around anymore
Gone, not forgotten
Belief – God opened the door
Our home place in Illinois
School we attended
In 1900 it was erected
Names mentioned
A book of history recommended
Country roads long ago narrow,
Could not meet nor let anyone pass
Of course those were horse and buggy days
No worry price of gas
Neighbors held races
Winner got a $5.00 pot
Inviting, exciting, riding
Or a team driving
Walk, race, gallop or trot
Those great horses
I used to braid their manes
Tie on ribbons to match
Color same as driver or rider
Then winner threw into crowd
For lucky ones to catch
Those days are gone forever
But fade from memory never.

# ANYWHERE

Dreams are for poets
One of a kind
Thoughts, ideas
They come from your mind
Sitting quietly
Or out for a run
Magic in writing
Where, what you see
Interesting tranquility
Traveling distance
Returning home
When complications unravel
Take time, write a poem.

# 12-25-07

A day for remembering
Someone alone
Wish a Merry Christmas
By computer, typewriter or phone.

## LIFE

Life will be wonderful
If doing your best
Educate, evaluate
Before stopping to rest.

## WISH

The way to travel
Costs minutes in your dreams
Lingering in mind
Real life not unkind
Remember mistakes, correct
You awaken each morn
Realize time passed
Remember who you met.

## WE

If we could ring
The bells of freedom
Set all countries free
Created by the Master
Wishing peace and harmony.

# QUIP

The moon is full of cheese
My neighbor said
Do you suppose
They eat crackers or bread.

# PATHWAY

Traveling life's pathway
Gather thoughts together
Gaze at blue skies
Clouds overhead
Float like a feather high
Time filled with joy
Musing memories
Days long ago passed by.

# PLACE

Everyone is wishing
Heaven's blessing to receive
If we're given the lower place
We would wilt
Like August's fall leaves.

# *BUGS*

Love bugs are coming
With the month of May
Leave a mess on windows, doors
Wherever you are
When not removed quickly
You will need a paint job
For your new car.

# AGE

When I was young
I loved to dance
Now at age 95
I'd be taking a chance.

# FLY

Did you ever wish
Like a bird you could fly
Perch like they do
View clouds floating by
Catch a snow flake
Falling to earth
Children making snowballs
Wish they had worth
Be young again
See a falling star
Ideas, dreams
Cost nothing, no pain
Sun, moon and stars
Forever will last
Keep on thinking
About time past.

# CREATOR

Master using knowledge
No extraordinary lessons

People asking questions
Cost of today's college
Today, why?
Humanity tries to conquer space
Would there be room
All to live everyplace
Centuries long gone
Produced food to serve
Planet earth feed
Money spent exploring
The devastated could be free
Agree
Live in our world
Everywhere on earth
Difficult to understand
Suffering hunger
Places of their birth.

# INTERSTATE 95

Going on a journey
On U.S. "95"
One of the great highways
From north to south
Far and wide
Cities, mountains
Oceans, rivers
We drive, while planes fly
Coast to coast and
To foreign nations
All over the world
Each offer welcome
But I like USA most.
Restaurants excellent
Good food
Everywhere
From Florida to the northeast
"95" will take you there.

# YES

Keep ideas busy
When you pause to rest
Busy hands, happy heart
Always do what's best.

# FUN

Take time to meditate
On your yesterdays
Seeing happy people
Traveling super highways
Where do they go
What did they see
Did all enjoy scenery
Would rather be happier
Climbing a tree
Children have ideas themselves
What is fun
Zipping around on skate boards
Riding bikes, going for a run
Soon they are adults
Lending a hand to everyone
When in need, come what may
Enjoying success any time
Night or day.

# *07-20-14*

A starry night
Rolling sea
Sand between toes
Happy and care free
Waves washing in
Memories unfold
Life still worth living
Years past
Stories untold.
Born in '14
Hope adding a few more
Trying to be helpful
Sometimes a chore
Enjoying surroundings
At number 10
Would it be worthwhile
To start over again.

# A SKETCH

Friends sending good wishes in 2007
Promises of being lucky
No money given places
In 2008, a note requests
Vodka, gas, vouchers or cash
Answer
Vodka may cover all bases
But if you drink too much
You won't be on the mend
But forget there's no money to spend.

# THEN AND NOW

The year 1933 has memories
My husband bought
The most expensive Chevrolet
Sedan, wire spoke wheels
Trunk on the rear end
Two spare tires, leather seats
Gasoline 25 cents a gallon
Oil then 40 cents per quart
How many years away
Will it take
Or who will remember
Prices of May 2008
Continuing to cause
Difficulties people cope with today.

# LEARNING

Thanks for living
Being forgiving
Lending a hand
Not on demand
Extended given
Wander at will
To the old saw mill
Pickup discarded pieces
Baskets to fill
Build a bird house
For a small boy free will
Present to him
At day's end
A small gift for a friend
Will you be happy
Growing up
His answer
I am pursuing education soon
Money might come my way
Building bird houses
For tomorrow's graduation day.

# *JACKY*

Our new Schnauzer pup
We'll call him Jacky
Busy as a bee
Inside outside
Roams the yard
Chases squirrels up a tree
Can jump like a kangaroo
On the bed
Up and down
Loves and chews
On my shoes
For a treat will
Put them down
Likes watching television
Especially viewing cats and dogs
Sits barking until they're out of sight
Many times will not obey
Although he went to school
Graduated top of class
Guess he needs a refresher course.

# SENSE OR NONSENSE

A song years ago
*'Jimmy Cracks corn*
*I don't care…"*
I wonder
Was he standing
Or sitting on a chair?


Q. – The difference between assignation and murder
A. – the spelling


Did you wonder many times
Why round pizza comes in a square box.


A game called
Pop Goes the Weasel
Was it something
To drink
Or part of an easel.

Why do people
Take the top floor
Then pay for binoculars
To look at the ground.


Vegetable oil comes from veggies
Corn oil from corn
Baby oil from babies?


Why do people give their "two cents worth"
If thoughts are only work a penny...

# CURIOUS

If the twinkling little star
Falls to earth from afar
Is the milky way
At heaven's gate every day.

# ODDITY

At a restaurant recently
I placed my order
Seated next to my sister
She said, I will have the same
After waitress departed
She returned saying
One of you needs to select something else
The cook will not serve the same thing
To two people at the same table
I asked, are you new here
Oh no she answered
I've been here three years
Her smiling reply
I can't explain or
Should I try.

# WHY NOT

A neighbor said
Life's not worth a dime
Not even a cent
So give me a nickel
It will be well spent.

## Tears

Little angel hear my prayer
For a happy day
Seeking smiles
Tears will go away.

# A WAVE

As good times unfold
You are never too old
Ninety-five is just a number
Wait and see
Return to thirties
Great times enjoyed
Worked outside
Helping others for free
Having box suppers
At the old school
Square dances
Fiddles, guitars, banjos
Music played just right
The piano belonged to
Teacher Ms. Margaret Puhl
Then locked up tight
All went home happy
A shake of the hand
Or a kiss on the cheek
Wave of emotion
See you next week.

# *JOHANNA*

Johanna Cobb
Went off to visit
Brother Jack
Carol, Kristine, Richard and Stephanie
We neighbors missed her
As did our Jacky.
And her "boys" Rascal, Scamp and Missy
Staying home they want to take a walk
Greeting people along the way
Being taken care of by friend Sue
They enjoy but hope their "mommy" will
Hurry back on a beautiful sunny day.

British Airways in Orlando
Her starting place
Taking off for London town
Where she will visit friends from all around
Next destination Perth, Australia
With enroute stop in Dubai
After many hours in the sky
Met by Jack's family
To celebrate Kristine's graduation
Then all too soon, bye-bye.

Greetings with love to your family
Enjoy the celebrations Joan
On your return to Orlando
We will greet you when landing
Carry back to your home

# MEMORIES

I strolled the streets of Boston and Washington DC
Thrilled by the tour of the White House and Pentagon
Visited the monuments of our country
Toured San Francisco, Los Angeles, San Diego
Long Beach, the Queen Mary and Spruce Goose
Then down to Monterey
Via the Pacific Highway
Can't forget Palm Springs
All inspiring
Ships and yachts everywhere
Anchored in the bay.
The Atlantic and Pacific and islands in between
Mined for diamonds in Aruba
Even played a game called Gin
Then was time
Returning home to Illinois
A beautiful holiday
Remembering experiences
Sights so much enjoyed.

# *SYNC*

Having wondered many times
If my mind is out of sync
Trying to capture memories
Before going *kerplink*
Should I worry when dawn brings a new day
Or do as I please
Let my ideas stray
Mind at ease.

# THINK

Were you walking alone
A trip of thoughts unpleasant
Consider child to adult grown
Thinking of family
Neighbors down the road
When needing help everyone willing
Ease a heavy load
During draft of World War II
Say young were called to assist
Willingly aid our country
Tears shed, a goodbye kiss
Now, as then we keep on wishing
Prayer, musings atone
Answer a multitude of hope
For thousands alive will be coming home.

# SUMMER

Traveling highways
Watch the sun rise
Put a smile on your face
Blue skies, butterflies
Your surprise
Summertime
No need to clean the fireplace.

# WINTER

Wintertime sharing enjoyed
Colorado, Utah, Maine, Wisconsin state
All great evenings
The lodge, a stein in hand
Pleasure, why hesitate.

# PAY

A time to live
Take a chance
Pay the piper
Plan a future in advance.

# *NOT ALONE*

Having written poetry and songs
Through many years
Brings memories to surface
Laughter, smiles, tears
May we talk with one another
Pain, sad feelings stray
Fill days with pleasure
Say a prayer each day
We have much to treasure
Angels lead the way.

# *EFFORT*

Life has made me realize
My musings unfold
Past times behold
Kindness to fulfill
A note of thanks, good will
Encouragement, admiration
Waking up generosity
During good deeds
Say Hi, hello, howdy
A pat on the back
With chance to succeed
Give thoughts of inspiration
For efforts you put in it
Remember days of happiness
Never have a limit.

# RULE OF THUMB

Travel not in terror
Life shows a better way
Moon and stars in splendor
Evoke happiness each day
Someone watching waiting
Messages from those you love
Create admiration
Blessings from above
Everyone has problems
Whether old or young
My dad used to say
Remember, tis the "rule of thumb"
Seek unhappy people
Share a handshake, smile
Angels whisper secrets
Make life worthwhile.

Traveling east
Going west
Remember always
Mistakes are a mess.

# WHY NO REPLY

A lonely road
A heavy load
Back pack shown
Question asked
Need a ride
Answer I have no home
May we help you on your way
That would be great
Saying we would stop to eat and rest
Oh, that's first rate
And would be best
My life will be lonely now
Dad and mom are gone
I hope someone will greet me
Three times in Iraq
Now my wish for you
Happiness
You had a life of hell
Make new friends
Live, let old memories
Help recall good things
Where you always did well.

# SEED

Seed planted
Enchantment granted
Share happy days of living
Forget yesteryears
Tomorrow is coming
Be generous forgiving.

# HELP

Date is June 28, 2008, time 4:45 afternoon
The wind began, thunder blasted
Lightning stuck our home
Causing disaster
Fortunate no fire
But looking into the attic
A large hole through roof in sight
Letting in daylight
Rain came in
Causing damage not good sight to see
But thanks to blessed neighbor
Who patched temporarily
We'll remember always Kurt
For his kindness and generosity.

# IDEAS

Dreams are for poets
One of a kind
Thoughts, ideas
Where they come from
One's mind
Sitting quietly
Or out for a run
Magic in writing poetry
Let's me happy be
Interesting tranquility
Travel distances afar
Returning home
Complications unravel
Take time write a poem
View someone unhappy
Use plan "B"
Interested acknowledgement
Is A, B, C
Always be careful
Pleasure, enjoy
Life is great
Anxiety, tension free.

# OKAY

Seek pleasure daily
Look for rewards
Keep mind and fingers busy
While inside or out in yard
Many times more burdens
Come as days arrive
Do not fret or forget
Prayers help us survive
Weeds in flower beds flourish
Grass in shrubbery
Cleaned out each day
Will grow back tomorrow
Seems they have the right of way.

# GONE

An interested speaker
Communicating fluently
Forgot what he was to say
An echo came from back of room
Spoke saying
Fluently just flew away.

# DEAR DAD

Son said
Dad I need a new golf club
Dad replied
I just gave you two
Son answers, I know dad
Yesterday I hit the ball so hard
Made a "hole-in-one".

# EASE

Seems many folks forget
We each have one life to live
Take time to wonder
What tomorrow might bring
Sunshine or showers
Ease for your sorrows
Fly away like a bird on wing
Pardon my suggestion
Creating a question
Some days end in a mess
Sure I regret them
Try to forget them
Another time confess.

# TRY CLIMBING

A mountain never reaching the top
Failing ear plugs, oh boy did my ears pop
Memories issue ideas
Leave years to explore
Give it a try
Enchantment follows
Days quickly pass by
Never reaching the pinnacle
Go down the other side
Streams below
Waters flow
Beautify countryside.
Try a smile
Do not frown
Find life
More worthwhile.

# REMEMBER

Precious are the hours
Things we accomplish each day
One issue reminds us
Take a few minutes to pray
Give a greeting to all you meet
Today September 11, 2008
Prayers said for those
That fateful 9-11 date
We remember they were martyrs
Gracious God has them in heaven.

# *HUMOR*

A new teacher was trying to make use of
Her psychology courses.
She started her class by saying
"Everyone who thinks they're stupid, standup!"
After a few seconds, Little Tommy stood up.
The teacher said, "Do you think you're stupid. Tommy?"
He ever so sweetly answered
"No, ma'am, but I hate to see you standing there
All by yourself."

# HELP

Be thrifty
Do not squander
Decide not to wander
Please stay close to home
Take time to share
A minute of prayer
Anger and pain overcome
Love, live, willingly forgive
Days follow one by one
Power care, saying a prayer
Will help day by day
A heart filled with hope
No longer mope
Let sunshine fill each day
Makes living worthwhile
Smiles are in style
Let pain suffered stray.

# THANK YOU GOD

Twenty inches of rain
Caused everyone to complain
We suffered wind and water
But no hurricane in our area
Thank you God once more
Easing agony and chore
You closed the door
Kept us safe
Through prayer we implored

# WEATHERING THE STORM

After six days being house bound
Having breakfast on the lanai again
What a pleasant way
To begin our day enjoying hibiscus
Peach and scarlet red
Flowers, shrubs blooming
Seemed to bow their head
After twenty inch rainfall in sadness
Though sent from heaven
At tremendous cost
Many people's home lost
It was no hurricane
Just severe tropical storm
Terrible flooding causing fear and pain
Interrupted schools and business
But faith holds us and
The sun will shine again.

# WISH

Did you ever make wish
Though foolish it might be
Beautiful clothes, shoes
At age of thirteen
Working for five dollars a week
Wish more money you could get
Wishing a dream
Some days passed quickly
Especially at laundry time
The most difficult
Hanging outside on the line
Wish you could go shopping
Money paid back then
Most less than a dime
Wish someone you meet
Could go to a movie
Get ticket for twenty-five cents each
Sack of popcorn extra
Back then that was groovy
Have time on your hands
Start writing poetry
Usually in the evening
After eight o'clock
Nights were free
Wish when you get older
Find one to share life
Store wishes daily
Lasting many years
Wish happiness
Never disappears

My wish for youngsters today
Start wishing while young
Wish for contentment
As life goes on.

# THE BEST

Embers glow when fire is low
After a fun filled party
Memories bring back happy times
Especially those on SR 40
Family days
Long highways keep us far apart
From California to Texas
Where to start
My kids, grand children.
Great grand and great-great
Grand children scattered all about
Don and Rita
Karen, Rick, Tim, Denny, Tricia
Chelsea, Callahan, Joe and Stephanie
Add Chase and Maddison
All from the Kunzweiler clan
May they all be successful
Accomplished with dreams come true
According to God's plan
Have memories, live with pride
Happiness the right answer
I pray angels walk by their side.

# A PAUSE

Did you ever pause like me
Realize the many footsteps you have taken
It would be like counting stars
Night times when I awaken
The many pathways trod each day
Whether running the Hoover
Walking around the pool
When young
Dance, run, exercise
Swim, play ball, with five brothers
That's when all things were cool.
They are gone now
I am much older
So take life in stride
Help needed many ways
Depend on my guardian angel
To aid me, be my guide.

# YOURSELF

.

Never falter
Sincerity walks along with knowledge
Something you learn each day
Will help you in college
Anger must not bother
If not passing the test
Next time be encouraged
Tell yourself
Do my best
Live and learn to justify
Choose the road you take
Encouragement given your future
Make it great.

# KNOWLEDGE

The English language
Contains four words only
Ending with "dous"
Hazardous
Horrendous
Stupendous
Tremendous
So when you write
Show independence.

# *THINKING*

When you believe
Life is worth living
Say a little prayer
When hurt, be forgiving
Perhaps someone will care
You have much to share
Some people more important
Since the beginning of time
Trying to feel you belong
Really worth more than a dime
Live for today
Hope for tomorrow
Make each day worthwhile
Fill each with a smile.

# *WHY*

How many times in life do you feel
This has happened to me
In recent years, thinking back
Has been a long time things you mention.
Ideas make a question
When things important arise
That's a stupid suggestion
What do I invest in life
Each day as I awaken
My nerves are shattered in many ways
Path of life I have taken
So look at beautiful flowers in bloom
Don't fret a storm coming soon
With roar of thunder
Think of good times passed
And my years are just a number.

# *FLOODS*

No need to complain
The season June to November
If no hurricanes
Maybe floods to remember
Water comes down in torrents
Makes ocean, rivers, lakes and low lands overflow
Terrifies folks, damages their homes
We sympathize with them
Offer prayers for all affected
Give them courage and hope
And perseverance to cope.

# *EXTRA PAY*

Many people offer ideas
About a purchase bought
In a week was on sale
Not as good by second thought
Returning to purchase place
I gave a big holler
The fine print not read
Said items returned to display, restock
Cost a dollar

# *BURN*

The summer sun
Can cause a burn
On a sandy beach
When the tanning oil
Begins to boil
Painful lessons teach.

# THANKS

To the life guards
Let's give a toast
They save swimmers from the ocean
To them life means the most.

# OCTOBER

Soon it will appear
Cooler weather will add cheer
Halloween is coming
Costumes from angels to horrid ghosts
Young folks are happy
Most important the idea
Instant pleasure
Who collects candy the most.

# HOPEFUL

Thanksgiving Day is coming
Important to me
The end of hurricane warnings
May each happy be
Time passes rapidly
Year 2009 soon gone
Pray 2010 brings prosperity
Without fear and nothing wrong.

# NOISE FREE

Cycles are roaring in Florida
For races many folks to not like
Calling them noise makers
But
Having two brothers and three grandsons
Their bikes a man's world of fun
I used to ride with them
Hanging on tight
Every minute enjoyed
Except wheelies and sharp turns
They caused a bit of fright
Anytime you can visit Daytona
In February or October
The colors and styles so worthwhile
Sights to see everywhere
The fests now a world-wide affair.

# IT'S MYSTERIOUS

Life's mysterious
Each day we live
Impossible, expensive
Donations to give
Problems, money
People face everyday
Trying to cope
Saving in any way
Children unhappy
No dollars to spend
I wonder how soon
We prosper again
Education enormous
All think they need a car
Gas many dollars per gallon
Books cost terrific so far
Make blood pressure rise
Our nation in debt
Higher than the blue sky.

Think you're important
Here's my advice
Ignorant sayings
Not very nice.

# US

Musings give pleasure
Enjoy when tomorrow comes your way
Start with prayer
Love all you know
Sunny days
Great thoughts overflow
Celebrate.

# TAG OR BAG

Try being helpful
Be attentively kind
When effort blows your mind.
Sitting in front of me
A lady in church with a tag
Showing price she'd paid
Think she would be embarrassed
When walking down the aisle
Touched her gently saying
May I fix your tag
Immediately thank you was said
She fixed her bag
Untwisted the shoulder strap
Thanking me again she stated
I usually wear it that way.

# WINTER

November to March
Winter time in Illinois
Severe winds blowing
Temps get to ten below
Snow measures many inches
Covering your play hut
Breath from your mouth freezes
Cold makes you keep it shut
Sure I enjoy Florida living
Still loved Illinois memories icicles, snowballs
Back in the twenties
So many simple things to enjoy.

# THE FLETCHERS

Maureen and Greg
May you enjoy and treasure
When the books are read
You'll find pleasure
Bring memories of mom, dad
Remembering loving times we had
Now they are in heaven
Watching o'er us every day.

# GOD BLESS

9-11 terror anniversary
Twin towers were destroyed in New York
Horror the world to see
Authorities should have known
USA had been warned in advance
Danger was on the way
Ignored, preparations were not made
To keep USA safe
Thousands lost their lives
All God's creation
Billions gone
Why carry on
May each life lost have found God in heaven.

# BOOKS AND WORDS

I like music
And singing
Listen everyday
I have poetry
Written to words set to music
Not yet published
But soon I hope and pray
My two books of poetry
Beautifully done by *IUniverse*
Another (this one) in production
Will complete the trilogy.
Writing gives me pleasure
A grand pastime for sure
Guess I should get busy
Write one more to store.

# YES

If you drive lickety spilt
You have a crash
Say to yourself
Was a nice car
Until I got hit

# IT GETS COLD

When winter comes to Illinois
Freezing snow and ice
Icicles hang from everything
Listen to my advice
Zero weather freezes
Fingers, ears and toes
If not protected
Will even freeze your nose
Now a vow I must speak about
Being very bold
The outhouse in back
Golly gee, those seats were cold.

# 95 DEGREES

When summer comes
July and August best
No school to attend
That's when we took
A fresh egg from the nest
Just for fun
Tried frying it on the sidewalk
Cooked by 95 degree sun.

# GOOD DEED

Motivate one to think
What tomorrow might bring
Go to a level higher
Stimulate thoughts of early spring
Offer help if needed
Respect you will gain
Be not lax doing work
That comes your way
Like cleaning a closet
Giving items help
Someone use them
Will bring smiles your way
No more clutter
You'll accomplish things worthwhile.

# *WHEN BLUE*

May I whisper a secret
Hoping it will not stray
Just bring some happiness
As you travel miles away
Whistle a tune
Of happy thoughts
Make up words you choose
It takes just a few moments
When you have the blues
My day was good
The afterglow supreme
Tomorrow happiness returns
No more tears just another dream.

Greetings to one and all
Famous names, happy faces
Thanks are not enough
You're enrolled in God's graces.

# IN A NAME

We have names to admire
Marilyn, Travis, Johanna, Annie
Don B, Jack C, Gruber and Giganti
Clymer, Crowley, Dewey
Gottlieb, Grieme, Guney, Irene
Poschel, Padhe, Tom and Alexa
Margot, Masters, Munie, Morrison O'Malley
Sheehy, Scott, Fletcher, Kieser, McGhee
Stogner, Bradley, and Points
Bertrand, Ryan, Evans
Mike and McGhee
Then Haase, Morano, Grasso
Clarke, Chelsea, Markus
Schaeuble, Price, Helfenstein
Leo Ryan and Fran and Mick
VanderHeiden, Sorrell, Harman
Hansen, Alexander, Hamilton
Karen, Mercedes, Callahan
Sally, Beaver, Roger, Keiser
Stephanie, Tricia, Chase
Maddison, Dolores, Price
Ursula, JJ, Bob & Fran
The sum of these equals
A wonderful clan.

# A NEW DAY

A new day dawns
Great surprise
Greetings and pleasure
Brilliant blue skies
Neighbors going to work
Kids off to school
Shout hello
People like these
Their salutation
Warm and friendly
Tickles imagination
How lucky we are
With blessings bestowed
Be good to one another
Lest we're taken for granted.

# TOUCH OF LOVE

Finally reached my mind
Finding someone I could help
She was going blind
Took her to my doctor
Examination was no cost
Being shocked, mystified
She whispered
My aunt Minnie
For weeks she has been lost.

# DREAMER

I guess I'm a dreamer
Traveling like a gypsy
Offering a hand
People out of work
Employment scarce
Business closings everywhere
Many folks seem at end of rope
Asking help with abated voice
Children neglected
Schools consolidated
Teacher lay-offs
Add to problem
Price of food out-a-sight
Cost of basics a fright
Keep chin up and say a prayer
There's always someone who will care.

# NONSENSE

A small child asked me
"Want to know why my dad had to buy a new golf club?"

Because he made a hole in one.


Another one quips:

"The football player liked eating crackers at the super bowl!"


Some basketballs need suitcases because they travel a lot.


The teacher asked second graders to spell Kleenex
One smart little boy raised his hand and spouted  T – I – S – U

# # #
Sign at old Ashland Illinois Grain Elevator

*NO LONG WAITS*

*NO SHORT WEIGHTS*

# # #

# JUST WONDERING

Sometime you wonder
What a new day will bring
Flowers, shrubs, trees blooming
Red cardinals whistling
Tiny humming birds
Receive nectar
From the azaleas
The deer keep coming
Eat much vegetation each spring
May is getting closer
Tis then the love bugs arrive
June begins then
Hurricane time
We pray everyone will survive.

# KEEPING UP

Hibiscus bloom in glory
Magnify in beauty
They need care
Watering, feeding, weekly duty
Glories of magic surrounding
All at 10 Foxfords Chase
Living was great in Illinois
Many more things enjoyable
Being here in Florida
Now 13 years in 2008
It was great when I could drive
Going somewhere everyday
Unable to walk now
Without someone to aid
I must not despair
Days, weeks, months, years
Pass in review
Just keep busy
Eating out a treat
Breakfast, lunch or dinner
Some places we go great
Others just so-so
Loud music is a no-no.

# CLIMBING

Climbing to enchantment of life
Fell to the valley below
Landed on moss for a cushion
A million flowers in my hair
Arose from a moment of pleasure
Found I was not alone
Surrounded by angels with lamps
Raising me up music began
They all began to dance
Wearing crowns of flowers
Adorning their beautiful hair
Made me suddenly realize
I had no business there
One of my greatest
Dreams to behold
At my age of 94
There is a place for everyone
And one to open heaven's door.

# THE PROMISE

Some say there is a promised land
How far must I travel
Will days last a long time
My years to unravel
Saying oft times
Do you remember
Boggles the mind awhile
I wonder about heaven
Do angels wear a smile
Then another place we hear about
Far down below
Will we have chance to ponder
Who, when will ever know
Alive our thoughts may wander
Memories fulfill
We appreciate each day given
And try to do God's will.

# GREATER DAYTONA BEACH

Sandy beaches many miles
People travel by train
Ocean liner and plane
Not to mention car
Visitors come from distances far
We have sharks, alligators, manatees
Wild hogs, reptiles and deer
Beautiful Herons and Eagles I like best
Circling high seem very shy
Find a high place for a nest

We have fine educational institutions
Embry Riddle, BCU, Daytona State College and UCF
We're home of NASCAR and Daytona International Speedway
Famous golf courses, museums, fine dining
A brand new hospital and condos rising
Can be seen from Interstate 95
Luxurious hotels on the ocean
Our skyline but sheer delight
Come on down anytime
Much to see day or night.

# I LOVE THIS COUNTRY

People on TV, musicians
Playing pianos, organs, guitars
Cruising the ocean
Or paddling about
A surf fun for many
As they ride afloat young folks like many
Drive very fast
Do not worry
Price of gas
Take a ride down
Ponce Inlet way
The lighthouse beautiful
Is history today
Travel farther down the coast
Stay for a blast-off
Excitement the most
Then hop on the 528
If not too busy
Soon you'll arrive Orlando
And a must visit to Disney.

# RETURN

Clouds on high
Floating like feathers in the sky
Fair greetings of my family
A breath of fresh air
I'll be staying home
Roam no more
Visiting folks I know
Going back to wife and children
Faith and courage
Peace will overflow.

# MOM

Kindness gift offering
To your mother any day
Look for pleasure
If only out to play
Say, see you later mommy
Think about many things
She would always do
There will never be another
"Mom" my hat is off to you.

# SPRING BREAK

Summer is approaching
Warmer weather on the way
Spring break gives all students
A special holiday
May each be cautious
Driving anywhere
Carelessness can be costly
Life does have no spare
I will write a letter
To Chelsea, Joe and Cal
Take care my darlings
Remember life is worth it all.


# 52 QUIZ

What has 52 in counting
Numbers, letters used once in awhile
Never found in yards
Enjoyable hobby for some
A love of life for many
Entertainment
A simple deck of cards.


# EASTER

Easter time is coming
Each child expects a bunny
Be sure you buy one only
They way they multiply
Results may not be funny

# ACKNOWLEDGMENTS

Brother Leo Ryan
For regards sent
Thank you very much
Remembering you for many years
Don and I say keep in touch.

Father Jack O'Malley, blessed friend
Seems you're always on the go
When again down Florida way
Our welcome mat is on display.

Dolores Edwards ("Sis")
Find pages to enjoy
Most happy, full of pleasure
Others leave memories to treasure.

Shirley Kieser
An enjoyable day
You came with Kent to visit
Come back again for a longer stay.

Maureen & Greg
Galena is fine, Florida weather better
Come visit and see
Our hospitality is free.

Tom and Alexa
Come on down out of the cold
Time passes so quickly
Let's not get old.

Lynette & Jim
When you travel
Down Florida way
Next time stop and spend
More than just a day.

Theresa and Ernie
Wish you could visit
Where life is sublime
We'll host you anytime.

# PERSPECTIVES

## A TO Z

A – Action doing

B – Best of giving

C – Calling mankind

D – Do get involved

E – Each will reply

F – Forever gaining ideas

G – Giving people assistance

H – Hope someone listens

I – Idle time no demand

J – Joy keeping busy

K – Knowing all is well

L – Life worthwhile

M – Moments of anxiety

N – No chance to smile

O – Open your heart

P – Promise the ability

Q – Questions – ask!

R – Reality important

S – Sincerity simple task

T – Tell the truth

U – Understanding paramount

V – Value answers

W – Wisdom a virtue

X – Xylophone enchanting

Y – Your day melodious

Z – Zoology a science

# DIFFERENCE

He asked for a dime
You said I do not have
But give you two nickels
His answer
They aren't worth a penny.


*…Foolishness…*

*The Polish woman said*
*Do not wash the table*
*Polish it.*


*An assistant must*
*Realize he is not*
*To attend any invalid*
*His actions could be invalid.*

*.*


*A group of oarsmen*
*Got into a row*
*Before they started*
*To row.*


*You may not lead a group*
*Unless you get the lead out.*

*A farmer uses his produce*
*To produce.*


*The solider said*
*I found no dessert*
*In the desert.*

# PLEASE

I will not be blamed
My forgetfulness of anyone I know
If so I am sorry
Was that some time ago
Some of my days
Are very long
Nights are very dim
Memory short
Must write things down
That I need to report or quit
Do you ever get mail
Asking for money
In two weeks my mail box
Full with 21 of these requests
The hot sun made them gummy
I would like to give
And
Winning a sweepstakes would be grand
Just a dreamer me
For which there is no demand.

# THOSE DAYS

Unforgettable people
Memories entwine my heart
One of eight children
We never drifted apart
My father one of sixteen
Sisters and brothers
Once I could proudly claim
I had 164 first cousins
Aunts, uncles, others
States numbered many
New York, Missouri, Texas,
California, Illinois, Indiana,
Michigan, Georgia, Kansas
Family reunion many years ago
Numbered 340 by count
A photo I have a treasure
Many names, a large amount
I must not forget my memories
They keep me alert
Reporting each day
Enjoy while you may
No bad thought that could hurt.

# TAKE MY HAND

Take my hand trusted friend
We both have much to gain
May we rest awhile gather thoughts
A cup of kindness shared
Gives cause we both will smile
Wandering the path we traveled far
Night overtook with stars
The fading sun lowered in the west
How great this world of ours
Dawn arrives again
We walked many miles
Came to the cross roads of our journey
Dave reached out his hand
Mike answered come home with me
Mom said
They will meet us with a band.

# SERENE

The oceans wash the beaches sand
Gifted by God's hands
Seagulls soaring in the sky
The leader in command
Are you pursuing happiness
Remove obstacles away
Whisper messages to angels
They comfort from above.


Tis soon the leaves of autumn
Turn from green to red and gold
Squirrels gathering food for winter
Storing away from winter cold.

# PONDERING

If tomorrow is today
What happened to yesterday
Idleness gave me thought
About many things I bought
Give someone pleasure
A small token to treasure
Remembering back to golden history
Money would offend
Someone who was a special friend
A hanky would leave a memory
Not aiming to impress
Just a show of happiness
A friendship to last a lifetime
Wonderful, free.

Such a friend Don "Roger" Bacon
Who lived on Edwards Street
Way back then
School days were great
At old Sacred Heart
Remembering all attending
Good Franciscan nuns teaching
The best anyone could ever meet
They lived and taught the golden rule
Their school could not be beat.

# *TRIALS*

I wonder what's the matter with me
Maybe arthritis in my knee
Other things I wish to erase
Like the wrinkles in my face
Do not hear what people say
The darn aids in ears give me away
Use a walker to get around
Necessitates walking on solid ground
Sure I know my age is "old"
And will never have picture on centerfold
What a snap shot taken –maybe grim
Oh well, my poetry makes me begin
And a glass of wine keeps me thin.

# SAD TIMES FOR MANY

I know there is heaven
A place below called hell
What folks are suffering today
No jobs, cutbacks, loss of income
Their homes foreclosed
Unsettling and no place to dwell
Agony for families
Children unable to understand
Kindergarten to college
All need a helping hand
Everything more expensive
Especially at the grocery store
What's happened to the USA
Since the uncalled for Iraq war.

# THINKING

Remembering many people I have met
Times of fun and laughter
Precious gifts collected
Keepsakes like china dishes
I will have no regrets
From Springfield to Chicago
Boston to New York
Switzerland to Austria
Germany, England, Scotland, Italy
Many masters' works of art
In Venice gracious people
Visiting beautiful parks
Traveling is an education
The best for all to view
Read about many I visited
In books, newspapers
Watch the travel channel on TV
Relish every moment
Recalling sunshine and dew.

# TACKY

*A friend told me*
*The guest was not present*
*To receive his present*
*She said oh well*
*It made me laugh*
*Cause I only paid*
*A buck and a half.*

# HOST OF MEMORIES

Will comfort one in their sorrow
Talk about yesterdays
Kindness will ease their sorrow
The road of life
Not always happy
A new life one should create
Have someone in for dinner
New friends meet
Maybe go on a date
A fresh road to travel
Life is still worth living
Even though hurt and pain
Let sadness unravel
The someone you meet
Might feel the same
A message to explore
Happiness is forever
Only when God opens heaven's door.

# REALISM

Understanding thoughts about spending
Enjoy doing
Idea pursuing
Bring smiles of pure delight
You will make a wrong
Come out right
Happiness will follow
Do not delay
You will conjure
Thoughts of pleasure
When you begin another day.

# A YELLOW POLKA DOT?

Invited to a swimming party
She asked what should I wear
A two piece or full
Answer doesn't matter
Just don't be bare.

Amen

Remember God is watching
Learn before it's too late
Time comes for everyone
To try to open heaven's gate.

# OR WHAT!

The doctor said
I will have to wrap a bandage
To cover and protect the wound
So he wound tape saying
I wound enough to take
Good care of the wound.

# SONGS

Songs of gladness
Songs of sadness
Songs can leave a happy smile
Songs of jubilation makes life worthwhile
Songs of someone helping others
Bring happiness and sometime tears
Songs of inspiration ease many fears
Songs by many mothers
Singing lullabies
Songs of choirs singing
Lifting voices to the sky
Songs to ease heart aches
Of someone you love
May the angels help a burden
Singing praise in heaven above.

# TIME

Time is not for nonsense
Tis an offer for the essence
Do not waste a minute
Spend your time in clear meaning
That might offer a good feeling
Finishing tasks you begin
Creating something artistic
Gather ideas optimistic
The feeling being forgiving
Enjoy life in every way
In today's way of living
Gets shorter every day.

# OUCH

Pain echoes a message
Offers a remedy
Lighten a burden
No sympathy, try empathy
· Reach for help if in need
You are sure to succeed
Begin to feel pain free
Long live this memory.

# *PRIDE*

Dreams are like poetry
Where they come from
What to write
Creeping in your mind
Brilliant as stars at night
Progress is a message given
Many like to say its living
To me poetry is entertainment
Relaxing any time of day
Never feel disappointment
Just feel lucky you
Flying a flag
Of red, white and blue.

# MUSIC

Someone said to me
Did you see
The man at the piano
My answer you know
Would have been
A good show
Had the baritone
Been a soprano.


Oh No


A singer of note
Once wrote
Keep head erect
Don't twist your neck
Your false teeth may eject
Causing performance to be a wreck.

# GOOD DEED

Fill a balloon
With bills you assume
Let go to fly high
Tie a note to the string
Saying no need to reply.

# NONSENSE

I read the note
You asked me to read
It said
Tomorrow wear red.



A little boy said to me
See those birds flying south
Be quiet, don't make a sound
They might turn and leave something
In your mouth.



A man driving down a country road
Pulled over and stopped
A large bee landed on the wind screen
What's your problem he asked
My car ran out of gas.
The bee said, oh
I'll return in a few minutes with help
Soon arriving with swarm of bees
And after a couple of minutes passed
The bee commanded, start your engine
The man said what did you do
The answer
Filled your tank with
BP.

# LIGHTNING

A bolt of lightning
Struck our home on 6-28-08
Blew a big hole in center of front roof
A torrent of rain followed
Put out fire, our thoughts great
Then discovered quickly
No computer, phone,
And other electronics
Damaged sprinkler system
Rain had ruined ceilings
The more we looked we found
That massive hole in the roof
Had splintered everything around
Trying to get estimates
Not an easy chore
Seeking help to repair everything
Nothing like this misfortune
Ever happened before
We were not home
When the bolt struck
But coming home from 4 o'clock Mass
Many said you were lucky
A blessing not being home
Never question God's plan
The blast would have scared
The hell out of you both
Worse than a brain scan.

*Blessings come when troubled*
*An unknown good neighbor came to our aid*
*Kurt got on the roof in the storm*
*Applied a temporary patch*
*Referred a fine roofer*
*And other craftsmen for interior work*
*Everything fixed perfectly*
*Proving, there are always angels around us.*

# THE SUNSHINE STATE

Florida with sandy beaches
Wind blast waves ashore
Reaching many miles
Travelers from many places
Arrive by plane, train, ships and cars
Enjoying the ocean soon they hope
Go to museum and investigate Mars
Take a cruise to view
Eagles, alligators and manatees
Visit Embry Riddle and Disney
Travel many places
Ponce Inlet great to see
An abundance of attractions
Even the London Symphony
Daytona International Speedway
A grand display
And don't forget the new Dog Track
Cap your day with dinner
At Halifax Plantation or LPGA
We've much to offer
Plan to come and stay.

# MADDISON

Maddison is small
A loving child
Moving to Texas from Florida
The new change was quite a treat
She has a smile for everyone
At the school she attends
Makes friends with all new kids she meets.

Chase, her brother, in third grade
The change for him not so hot
Thinks he's the greatest
Wished he was back in Florida
Where he was a big shot
Soon will both realize
How great it will be
When Mimi and papa visit
They will be full of do and see.

# TRY

I enjoy your pictures
Your extensive research
My 95 years of living
I remember when
Attending St. Brendan's Church
Do you think some time
You will find the end
Appreciation, knowledge
From many you depend
Keep up your hope
Look back
Centuries, years
Receiving, answering questions
Bring all near
Good thoughts happen
Problems disappear.

# TRIP

Yesterday, today, tomorrow
A day, week, month, year
Has filed my life with memories
With barrels of cheer
Traveled on highways
We humans have pursued
Flown high in sky above
Sailed ship on oceans
My grandparents came from England
On a ship named "Germania"
The year was 1825
To a country they learned to loved long journey at best
A daughter died, was buried at sea
Difficult to express
On landing at Ellis Island
Hundreds packed in like sardines
After months on the ship
They were given chance to smile
Being treated USA style.

# *WHY*

When astronauts landed on the moon
What did they expect
Oceans, rivers filled with
With whales, manatees, sharks
Dogs, cats, birds as pets
Places to manufacture
Build cities homes, parks
We keep hearing
Man will live on the moon someday
Really do we care
The money expended for space exploration
Could help many in despair
Millions, billions, spent
Pockets filled, cash, greed
Think of those whose lives were lost
Was it worth the cost
I don't see the need
Let's forget what is on the moon
Help those living on earth
Educate children, give jobs
The multitude prove
What a trillion is worth.

# *BROTHERS*

Stormy days make me remember
Years past when young
My mom used to say
Wishing
When the rain stops
Tomorrow we will go fishing
Have some fun
Night time we made balls of dough
Flour, water to bind
Leave them overnight drying.

I could not put worms on my line
My brothers laughed at me
Many times but little did I care
They soon ran out of *brit* [worms]
Then asked, Ann will you share.

# LIFE – WHAT IS

A fragment of being among mankind
In a great world of faith and hope
Knowledge, reading, listening
Music and Liturgy
Sometimes challenging to
Members in many issues
Faith embraces many following
In footsteps of learning, helping
Fulfill dreams of each one's self
My entire life has always been
A love of writing poetry,
Setting words to music
For my own pleasure
Some songs were published
Old vinyl recordings made
None however were sold
Asking why, think not bold
Firm unknown in the marketplace
To me it made no sense
Their advertising simply a gimmick
I received no recompense
But alas I will include the lyrics
In this my third book
So well done by "I Universe"
Books One and Two produced with excellence
Fulfilled a dream for sure
Copies sent to friends and family
In Australia, Germany, Dubai and many in the USA
So should ever get an idea glisten
Have courage and believe

Say a prayer
The Lord of all will listen.

# *ECHO*

Come visit any time
You are down our way
The mat says welcome
Even on a bad weather day
The sun will shine tomorrow
We have little choice
When you yodel from the mountain top
Echoes return full voice
You will not find this
If traveling the blue ocean wide
Or flying high above
Echoing your ideas
Gracious living
Will last long abide
As skies are full of stars
Moon is there also
Smiles on everyone's face
Even all who are below
And fight in wars.

# GRATITIDE

Thank you God
I implored
Having reached the age of 95
Saying Good Morning
Angel be my guide
To live, enjoy year 96.

# LITTLE RACHEL HELEN

A gift from heaven
August 4, 2008
Rachel Helen Guney
Blessed be the day of her birth
And Nathaniel, Zachary, Benjamin
Love her dearly – no surprise
Grandma Peg and Grandpa Bob
Stacey, Ike, her mom and dad
Will make her life so sublime
Each day she will be giving
A day of thanksgiving.

# THINGS

Fragrant flowers
Majestic trees
Roar of ocean waves
Gentle morning breeze
Roll to shore with ease
Watch gulls overhead
Flying along the surf
Things God created
His pleasure
Ours to treasure

All may enjoy
Mother earth
Humming birds in back garden
Butterflies and bees
Deer in early evening
Eat everything they please
Dew on early morning lawn
Shines like emerald green
Rain comes down to moisture ground
Creates dreams supreme
Never will I squander time
But relish each day carefully
Life sublime
The Lord's generosity
Giving us a life by the sea.

# *GRIT*

Some days I'm thinking
No way can I make it
Then say to myself
Stupid thoughts
Shake off, have grit
Next day arrives
Face with a grin
Say to yourself
Not bad
For the shape I'm in.

# *FAITH*

Why do you worry
Realize
There are clouds
Along with blue sky
Love of life
Faith concern
Thought for others
Satisfaction earned.

# MARCH 2009

Days in one's life
We have said, "I wish"
Washing windows, laundry, sweeping
Clearing away remnants after mowing
With a blowing swish
A great time to realize
Some deeds not necessary here
Thanks to the Almighty
No snow shovel to carry
Nor icicles hanging from the eaves
Or sleet or ice to hamper travel
Instead we enjoy
Robins, Cardinals, birds of blue
Building nests everywhere
In March 2009.

# MIND

Tell your mind
Give caring a treat
Follow a road endearing
To everyone you meet
In the Fall when daylight gets short
Night time comes soon
But notice the stars
Like diamonds shining
Surrounding a beautiful moon.

# A GIFT

Falling on Christmas day 2008
Sitting quiet for a minute
A prayer said for help from God
Dear Lord no broken bones
Strength to rise
A whisper
Help from asking
Took a few short minutes
There is a master of everyone
Falling could be worse
When an injury happens
Thanks said
Maybe time to call a nurse.

# TAKING A PLANE

For travel

Shoes, minus socks

Jeans, shirt, sweater

You can unravel

I cast a decision

Easy, painless, free, choose

No more freebees

No peanuts, pretzels, soda

Water is free?

Remember clothes you choose

Are ones on your back they cannot lose

or

Just travel by car

Stay at home - wonder

Golly gee, how far tomorrow

Fill your gas tank full

Sky of blue

Clouds billowing white

Stars and moon shining

A glorious sight

or

Try a holiday, ocean liner

Have memories

No gas, it's our money

We're saving tonight.

# DOES IT REALLY MATTER

If you are 3 or 93
When young no problem
Old, golly it's just a number
Year 2009 the zinger
Way you spend a small amount
Buy one get one free
Help out the hungry
Clean out your pantry
Donate several kinds
A few different things
Think, but for the grace of God
This could have been for you.
And an adage of old
Whatever one gives
Is repaid tenfold.




Sending a letter
Costs 44 cents
Next time use a cell phone
That makes writing
No good sense.

# HOW DOES ONE COUNT

The years
From one to ninety-three
Recently a friend asked
Age is creeping
Remember you and me
Now they lift eye lids
Pull cheeks back
When wrinkles being to fold
Use "lipo" on your tummy
Thighs and do your nose
Many times I pondered
Would I like what I see
If reading book you
Turn the pages to read
Continued on page three
Thinking about what to do
How can they take
Away the numbers
From one to ninety-three.

# ANOTHER NEW DAY

Morning comes alive at dawn
We have a new day to explore
People rushing everywhere
Then wonder
Did I lock the door
Then ponder
Today's problems
Boggle minds of all
Will gasoline prices keep advancing
Groceries, all expenses
We wonder what's in store
Summer activities will cost more
Oh, stop worrying for a moment
Utter a prayer
Seek His guidance
The good Lord is there.

# *SPARKLE*

The sparkle in your eyes tell me
You live a beautiful life
Reaching out from afar
Day's rising from darkness of night
A dreamer of enchanted places
Will not carry a load but
View contentment
Never show resentment
Cause he walks to middle of road
Time to return
Whistling a happy tune
Throws a stone while traveling along
Watch ripples in the lagoon.

# WANDERING

On sandy beaches
Children flying kites
Weaving turns and swirls
Giving folks delight
When a kite decides not to fly
Leaves a child forlorn
Yet he keeps on trying
And soon it is airborne
He says it's the greatest
I have even seen
And I'm not going to stop
Until some hollers
How 'bout an ice cream!

# *NATURE*

Do you ever say Good Morning
As a greeting to one walking
Every day see a smile
Give pleasure along your way
The sun will shine brighter
You will be delighted
Your hour brighter
Nature bubbled
Lifted thoughts to swing and sway
Power of your greeting
Brought sparkle to one's mind
Ease a troubled heart
Sure a day's good start.

# MAJESTIC RAYS

Magical days recalling
Smiles will cure
Memories worth sharing
Friends of long ago
Excitement grows
Happy times overflow
Steve and Marilyn return
To Chatham, Illinois
May they return next year
Enjoy more days of pleasure
Memories to treasure
Tomorrows pass quickly
Yesterday all gone
Look forward
We laugh and sing a song.

# *KK*

Kathleen and Kenny came to visit
The year 2009
Enjoyable memories
Made the best of limited time
Kathleen's dad my brother
Dorothy was her mom
We pray for both in heaven
As each day moves along
Thinking back time unravels
May all live a happy life
Take more time for travels
Avoid pain and sorrow
With a future of joy not strife.

# *JOEY*

Great grandson Joe Clarke
Enlisted in the Coast Guard
A handsome young fellow
Makes me very proud.
First off to New Jersey
The rigors of basic fine
After graduation his assignment
To the gulf coast of Mississippi
I hope to visit him there
Meanwhile I'll keep in touch
With love and daily prayer.

# USA

Loving our great country the USA

The sound of activity

Beach busy as ever

Memorial Day is celebrated

During a weekend every May

My wishes for all employment

If leaders everywhere cooperate

Find solutions to the many problems

Let us all say

Prayers everyday

Bringing our troops home

Would be a worldwide reunion

A celebration

Enjoyed by all not just our nation.

# A LINCOLN

A friend gave me a penny
My surprise
Is this a joke
His answer
Absolutely not
Keep it and you will
Never be broke.

# ECHO

I called across the mountain
My voice came back to me
Good morning sunshine
Aren't you glad today
Your echo leaves memory
Laughing, singing
God Bless America
No one around to hear
The sun is gone
My day is done
It's a quiet atmosphere.

# EASE

Resting on your laurels
A sign you have naught to gain
Glorify in honor
Have ideas for someone
A chance for fame.

# SELF CENTERED

Never be mundane
Give each day "Try"
Reach the peak of gravity
Like stars and moon on high
Be enjoyed by majority
Hold happiness close
Kind thoughts cherish
Keep gossip shuttered
Or conversation will perish.

# *LOVING*

Embers glow when fire is low
After a fun filled party
Memories follow
Happiness, joyful times
When all are together
Next time invite
All friends and family
A special niece from Texas
Dearest Ruthie
I would like to see
Refresh old memories
Enjoy the beauty
Keep in closer touch
We all share much
Visit when they can
May all have happy lives.

# HOPE

Our land of plenty diminished

Leaving families astray

Hearts breaking, little sunshine comes their way

Children disappointed

No camp vacation this year

Entire world in a mess

Anxiety, worry creating fear

Small children do not understand

Price of milk, eggs, bread, orange juice

Mothers and dads do the best they can

Money spent in billions

For what

Not lives to spare

May a new administration

Keep, grant promises

Work for mankind everywhere.

# JUST TRY

Every person has listened to someone
Speaking nonsense
Leaving reasonable doubt
Questioning an answer
The idea for you to decide
Talk like this very boring
I really cannot abide
Means their life has been dull.

Encourage them a moment
Suggest they smile
Your deed, good will
May help them to act better
Cause a miracle
No more idle time fulfill.

# *OKAY*

A bottle of beer
Or Glass of wine
A song of cheer
Happy time
Day at church
Dream fulfilled
Making one happy
Takes no skill.

# *WITH LOVE*

Many people wishing the Lord
Sends blessings from above
May countries have great leaders
Showing they care
May prayers be answered
With abundance to share
Keep families happy
Where ever they live
Continue pray, forget – forgive.




My third book is coming
With hope I thrive
My reason
07-20-09
I celebrated age 95
A prayer of thanksgiving
Life filled.

# THINKING ALOUD

If I leave behind a memory
My wish, someone will say a prayer
I would like to have an echo floating
Reaching all over the land with care
All would find happiness
Miles across our country wide
May all live lovingly
Walk harmoniously side by side.

# INTO THE AIR

Blow some bubbles
If in trouble
Soon they disappear from view
Like promises some people make
A balloon soon breaks
What's left, adieu!

# IN OUR ONE ROOM SCHOOL HOUSE

Songs we sang in school
Especially in the morning
The teacher said no shouting
That is a final warning.

Those old songs will live forever
Unlike the noise of today
Just close your eyes for a moment
Try to remember these, the joy will stay.

There were four in particular
Our teacher taught us to love
We remembered every stanza
Like gifts from above.

**America the Beautiful**
*By Katharine Lee Bates*

**Yankee Doodle Dandy**
*By Richard Shuckburgh*

**Home on the Range**
*By Dr. Brewster M. Higley*

**You're a Grand Old Flag**
*By George M. Cohan*

The words to these are still alive
Though seemingly seldom heard
If you want a quick refresher
Google is the word.

# *WHAT IS POETRY*

Only words on paper
Why I wonder
Well, why not
Print them for wall paper
Some could be fancy
Many bring a grin
A few might give a message
Cause a chance to smile
One alone might be okay
Could make a song
Or give reason to dance better
Maybe an offering
Like a real go getter
Hip-hip hooray
The old fiddle play
Serve the home brew
A jug or glass or two
Nothing could be better.

# HAPPENINGS

Sending some lyrics to
Horizon Music
With hope some favor
Will come in sight
Months passed with no acknowledgement
Nor response of any kind
Just like nearly 40 years ago
Their action is hollow.
One song in tribute to my brother
Served in the Marines
Landed on Iwo Jima
Told the story of those
Who came home from that war
To live in peace they had earned
Now most are in heaven
Probably aware of the Middle East mess
Hopefully asking their redeemer
World peace is soon blest.

# *WHEN*

When bells start ringing
War is at end
Our world will sing
Praising peace
It's grand to sing again.
Many lives lost
A gigantic cost
For freedom to live without pain
Family, friends, relation
May all be forgiven
Lasting pride to all who died
To our God we ask
Watch over the rest
May they be blest
Make a place for all in heaven.

# AHEM

Everyone asking for donations
Loading box of unread mail
I would like giving all a boot
I guess they would put me in jail
Sending notice to post office
To remove my address and name
The postman told me
To advertise, it's a game
In the last month
I had to buy a new shredder
Getting rid of the junk mail
Would make daily chores better.

# *HISTORY*

The top of the world
Appears to be Mount Everest
(Chomolungma) in the Himalayas
29,208 feet high
Although not a history buff
When a young girl I remember reading
Tibet was often called
"The rooftop of the world."
Seems it was difficult to reach
A mystery by all means
Makes one wonder
If it is still the same.
Surrounded by mountains
The bowl-like valleys
Lie in the midst of creation
These areas of the world
The hottest place known to man
In summer 120 degrees
Famously known "Place of Fire".

# BACK THEN

Old books were a hobby
Like old songs we used to sing
If we did that now
At my age ninety-five
Young folks would loudly cry.

To me nonsense is their thing
Loud acid rock and rap
Sad and disgusting
I need a sound proof door.

# SHARING THOUGHTS

Life is important
Living a delight
Laughter gives happiness
Learning what is right
Liking someone special
Looking back through the years
Lounging gives comfort
Listening for loud cheers
Leaning on someone you know
Lullabies you sing
Lurking around the corner
Are memories of spring
Lightning strikes, thunder roars
Loneliness might follow
Lunch will make you happy
Liberty is special - swell
Lasting many years
Little jokes you might tell
Later in the day
Sometimes just pray
Lookout for the angry person
Lye kills bugs, keeps them away
Leprechauns are Irish
Like twinkling stars at night
Lilies beautiful flowers
Livingstone a famous playwright.

# *1969*

Reading from a book I found
Dating back to 1969
Seemed silly things were quoted
Took me to older time
When a storm was brewing
We would open the barn door
So our farm animals were out of danger
Chickens hit the roost
Geese, ducks clattered much more
Dogs, cats and the parrot
Barked, meowed, parrot went
From cage to the floor
Rain came down in torrents
Covering the thirsty earth
We were happy when it stopped
Running through puddles laughing
Moistening everything for all with mirth.

# MAYBE

Pride goes before a fall they say
Many feel they are better
To me everyone is the same
Why must they think they're better
I could say my ABC's backwards
Count to one hundred when only 3
My two older sisters taught me
Their tutorship was free
Our father read our hero
Our exam questions
Our answers if mistakes made
We would have to do over
Twenty five times each one over
Before teachers would review
Questions to answer grade
All written on blackboards with chalk
Quiet time made
Followed a penalty if you talk
How great the memories
1918-1930 years go
Like chimes in a cathedral
Or winter white with snow
Yes memories
Like heaven on earth below.

# *AMERICA*

Our emblem
Old Glory
Known as the red, white and blue
Flying over the USA
The land I love.

There is a song
By George M. Cohan
Sang through the ages
One people will remember
Even with yellowed pages
*A Grand Old Flag.*
When I was young
We sang songs in school
Each day a favorite like *"Illinois"*
By the rivers gently
Flowing, Illinois, Illinois.

Now days are so different
No time for simple joys
The youth, girls and boys
Preoccupied with computers,
IPOD's, MP3s, l-phones and texting
Inventions with good intentions
But can detract from one's attention
Causing great risk - should we wonder
Hope these instruments
Will make for a brighter life
But maybe better if a
Return to magnificent basics
Listen to hear a drum and fife.

# *JACKY'S FRIEND*

We have a squirrel
Every morning
Runs across
The top of our pool screen
From west to east
Always the same routine
Unafraid of our Schnauzer
Just wanting to antagonize
As if trained by squirrel rule
Sits on the south east corner
Swishing his bushy tail
When Jacky starts barking
His friend jumps from screen to tree
Squirrels don't talk but this one chatters
As if to say
I can also fly like a bee.

# MOTHER NATURE

We read about tornados
Roaring across our land
And earthquakes
Around the world
Causing great anxiety, fear
Loss of life, pain and agony
People losing all they own.

Living in Florida
There is cause to fear
Hurricane "season" lasts
May 'til November every year
When tropical storms are forecast
To come our way
Should we stay home, or go away
Find a safer place
Will follow advice of authorities
But to the good Lord continue to pray.

# *KURT*

Late Saturday afternoon
On June twenty-eight
The year 2008
Lightning struck our home
On Foxfords Chase
The force blew a huge hole
Center top of our roof
Result of course, a fire
Pouring rain extinguished blaze
Before damage could be higher.

Panic – what to do
God sent Don to a neighbor
Kurt, a kind and gentle friend
Responded, ready to labor.
Patched the hole
Referred us to a capable roofer
Joe came Sunday morning
To assess and schedule needed repairs.

In today's world so full of distraction
It is rare to find people dependable for action
But here with wonderful neighbors like Kurt
Living all around
Such kindness can be found
A true blessing indeed
For a friend in need.

# *GRANDPA'S POEM*

A precious one from us is gone
A voice from us is stilled
A vacant place in our home
Which never can be filled

God in his wisdom
Has recalled his love had given
And through the body buried here
His soul is safe in heaven.

Grandpa died 11-21-1887.

# MY PARISH

*Saint Brendan's Catholic Church by the Sea*

Spiritual beauty abounds
In everything that surrounds
The magnificent main altar
The Guardian Angel chapel
The icon of our blessed mother
The Last Supper stained glass window
The great pipe organ
The outreach programs
The excellence of the school
All dedicated to the greater glory of God
Enhance one's ability to pray
In this beautiful house of worship.

I frequently attended St. Brendan's
Beginning in the seventies
When visiting my daughter and grandchildren
Until becoming a resident in 1994.
Now no longer a visitor but member
Of the church by the ocean
I thank Father Ryan and Father Queen
For their complete devotion.

# HIGH SCHOOL

Reading about a graduate
A few years long past
Susan Wright the writer
Proves time goes by too fast
Telling about her studies
At Father Lopez High
Fond, inspiring memories
Should go down in history
Encourage each and every student to try
Those formidable years
Pay rich dividends for they who apply
I believe that each attendee
At the new Father Lopez High
Will have an angel watching
From heaven's keeper in the sky.

# A SONNET

I was going to write a sonnet
One morning about the dew
There was a rabbit in the yard
In Florida we see very few
Made me stop and wonder
Was a child's pet on the loose
He didn't seem a stranger
Hopped looking around
Spied a patch of clover
Mowed it to the ground.

And I'm reminded of another feature
Beauty abounds in this creature
As the deer nightly arrive
Silently on the Hibiscus to thrive
A blossom first, leaves next
Then tender shoots, sakes alive
When finished, plant is done
Their hunger satisfied
The white-tails have won.

# *HOME*

Whistle a tune
Look at the sky
Watch white clouds
Floating on high
Hear birds chirping in windblown trees
Glory of living found in these.

Say hi or hello
To a neighbor working in the yard
Trimming shrubs, bushes
Gives oneself reward
Keeping things beautiful
About where you live
Remembering all ways
Great pleasure to give.

Pavers on driveway
Also on deck of pool
Adds touch of elegance
Looks mighty cool
Lawn mowed neatly
Danny does it weekly
Looks like a show case
Where we live on Foxfords Chase.

# PROMISED LAND

Some say there is a promised land
How far must I travel
Will days last a longer time
Take my years to unravel
Oft people say
Fran, do you remember
Boggles my mind awhile
I wonder about heaven
Will angels wear a smile
There is the other place
Which is far below
Will all have a chance to ponder
Will we succeed so
On bended knee
Who might ever know
If we reach that promised land
God mysteriously holds out his hand.

# EASTER 2008 – MARCH 23

*Trivia*

Do you realize
The next time Easter will
Be celebrated on March 23
Will be the year 2228
219* years hence

*written in 2009

Beautiful day
The 25th of May
Enjoy the beaches
Waves, washing to shore
Say a prayer
That the war will soon be o'er

# *AHEM*

When friends offer ideas
About a purchase
I bought
Reading direction
Not as good as I thought
Returning item to store
Caused me to holler
Putting back
On shelf
Cost me an extra dollar.

# *PEOPLE REMEMBERED*

07-20-08

My special day brightened by special friends:
Dewey, Bro. Leo Ryan, Peg Scott, Toyi & Ron, Ursula & JJ, Peg & Bob
VanderHeinden, Maureen, Mick & Fran, Sharon & Mark, Joe & Annie,
Theresa & Ernie,
Barbara & Dwight, Bill & Bennie, Sis and Jim, Charlie & Charlotte, Aldo
& Ginny, Roger,
Terry & Missy, (San Diego, CA), Timo (Mallorca, Spain), Sascha (Bremen,
Germany)
Stacey & Ike (Dubai), Sally & Red, Joan, Margot, Ruth & Ken (Conroe,
TX)
Tom & Alexa, Dick & Betty, Marilyn & Steve, Harlan, Tom Cruse, David
McGhee
And all the family.


To these and those whom I've missed to list,
My family, friends, neighbors
Known for many years
Through happy and sad times
Smiles and tears
Your phone calls, e-mail, cards, flowers
Words of cheer
My life still good at ninety-five
Makes one feel great
Wake to a day of sunshine
Keep mind sharp, alert
Pray if unhappy
Make no issue of hurt
My book
Line for you I will insert.

# IDLE TIME

Having thoughts about creation
Strange emotion came to mind
Does heaven have an ocean
Sandy beaches where thousands get a tan
Enjoying sunshine, playing ball
Have cars and busses
Going to the mall
Or is heaven restricted
Strange how thoughts come to mind
Guess when one writes fiction
Has imagination, too much idle time
In need of benediction.

# EXPEDITE

The path of life
We travel everyday
Angels ease the burden
Happy moments stay
There is danger the world over
Leaving pain if led astray
Countries full of torture
Need protection come what may
Use an ounce of energy
Loving not a loss
One who gave his all
Carried a heavy cross
Angels watching
Kindness showing
Expedite messages
For each every where
When we do our share.

# A THANK YOU

*I want to dedicate this page*
*To each and everyone*
*May you enjoy this book*
*My third*
*I hope you get some pleasure*
*From writings I treasure.*

*May the good Lord bless and keep you*
*Each and everyone.*

# GOOD FRIENDS

Time is of the essence
For my "Quarter Queen"
When the next one is available
I never have cause to fret
Bennie will deliver
Doesn't miss a bet
She and Bill
A caring pair
And look at their home
Easy to see they care
The surroundings
Landscaped as a sprawling garden
Manicured lawn and shrubs
Carefully planned variations
Shows all given solid consideration
Everything done with precise skill
I have lots of admiration
For Bennie and Bill.

# NEVER LAND

Where is never-never land
Land of milk and honey
Atop some mountain
Or maybe on earth
Where it's sunny
Could be deserts of sand
Or in the heavenly sky
The depth of oceans
Planes flying high
We believe in the Almighty
Like *Winken-Blinken-Nod*
In submarines exploring
Creation gifts of God.

# SEEK & FIND

Dreams of everlasting memories
Wandering humans on the earth
Seeking a rainbow fortune
Soon learn what is money worth!

# *GOOD DAY*

Good morning

Good night

God bless you

Said with delight…

How are you

A question, not demand

Might be

Who gives a damn?

Try being cautious

Offer a smile

While saying to yourself

Thoughtfulness

That's worthwhile.

# WHAT TO DO

Should you smile
Give a nod or grin
Show all
The mood you are in.

# TODAY

Today, Tomorrow, Yesterday
A day, month or year
One day is here next one arrives
The others disappear
We not will forget months of twelve
At times seemingly last forever
Then comes next year
365 days
Count them
Could bring pleasure, happiness
Pain or a tear
Having lived many of these
I still have peace of mind
Thoughts of life at ninety-five
Truly worth the time being alive.

# GRAM & GRAMP

My grandma Ruth
And Grandpa John
Born 1825
In jolly old England
But their dream
America!
With God at their side
They came to the USA in 1855
Landed at Ellis Island
Experienced agony like torture
Learning to become citizens
But took it in stride
Realizing their 30 days at sea
Actually easy to abide.
Finally settling in Illinois
Provided their big family much joy.
Thank you grandparents
I still pray
Remembering memories and love
Given by the good Lord above.

# APHABETICALLY SPEAKING

A – Be assiduous as you go along

B – Be brave to keep you strong

C – Be cautious, careful, show concern

D – Be daring at times, show surprise

E – Be eager, come what may

F – Be fun loving and fashionable everyday

G – Be gregarious, generous when helping

H – Be honest, have a plan

I – Be interested, intense

J – Be judicious, show common sense

K - Be kind and caring

L – Be loquacious, laugh, shout hooray

M – Be modern in style

N – Be never naughty

O – Be only yourself

P – Be patient and proud of the virtue

Q – Be quick to help others

R – Be reliable when asked for a favor

S – Be sensible in adjusting covers

T – Be truthful always to one and all

U – Be understanding answering a call

V – Be vigilant, live and learn

W – Be wise, watchful snot wayward

X – Be xerographic, make copies of your plans

Y – Be youthful, young at heart

Z – Be zealous in all endeavors.

# KNOW HOW

The little boy came home from school
His mother asked
Did you learn something today
No not really he responded
Explaining
The teacher asked
Does anyone know how to spell cat
I raised my hand
Said, C –A-T
Thank you she said but
I wondered why my teacher
Didn't know how
When it only took three letters.

*Anonymous*


A good friend told me
I'm going away
Asking where are you going
He said, I'll know tomorrow
When tonight's dream tells me
May I your luggage borrow.

# *TRAVEL*

Being me who loves to travel
By plane, ocean liner train or car
Distance traveling and security
Benefits all to agree
Use splash of Holy Water
On the car and your purse
Enjoy miles of pleasure
Troubles leave on a shelf
One thing to remember
Watch speed and be alert
Besides being injured
Your purse can also be hurt.

# 'CANE SEASON

Soon time is important
Now blue horizon is high
Clouds of white
Across a majestic sky
Lawns, shrubs green as emerald
Flowers blooming
Hibiscus peach, yellow, red
Sometimes offer a message
Of storms we all dread
Winds a very strong alert
Hurricanes cause damage, pain, hurt
Ocean goes on rampage
Rain falls in torrents
Be aware, all prepare
Flooding everywhere
If evacuated items take
Everything owned is at stake.

# ANOTHER DAY

Each morn when arising
I thank God and pray
Help me have a happy day
Keep me from saying something
Anything improper could show
The mind in disarray
Being older the time wanders
Disappointment interferes
Causing sadness or pain
Result in no gain
Views relax, keep quiet
Let silence play a part
My burden is not heavy
Found is easier to carry
With joy in my heart
An angel at my side
Acting as guide.

# JANUARY

January in Florida gave some funny weather
Heavy clothes, boots, gloves and muffs
A few more pounds to carry


Freezing beautiful shrubs, ferns lawns
Causing people anguish
Unusual storms, cloudy days
Everyone noticing, *"It is cold!*
*Are we in Florida*
*The sunshine state."*


But there is hope around the corner
Unlike a northern winter
The gloom is soon over
Looking to near future
Spring will bring peace of mind
Happy time, bright sun will shine
Then good ole summer time.

# A GIFT

Let your mind wander
Of memories every day
Thinking many give happiness
Stacked on shelves
For the merry month of May
Erase anger you had hidden
Feel better, come on smile
The grace of God will help you
Make your life worthwhile.

# TIME TO SEEK

Did I wonder
Not thinking how far would I go
Trying to solve a problem
As the sun lost its glow
Darkness followed quickly
Moon and stars began to show
Memories caught up thoughtfully
I am only ninety-four
Ideas dreams gracious living
Life has given me one day more.

# *PENSIVE*

What is fame or fortune
Does it create a throne
Pain when alone
A path of life if greedy
Little help for the needy
When many lose their home
People by millions
Saw the light of day
Elected a new president
To lead the right way
His name will go forever
Engraved in history
Give the USA chance to once again prosper
That will be his legacy.

# FRIVILOUS/ANNONYMOUS SIGNS EVERYWHERE

### ON A REPAIR SHOP DOOR
We can repair anything.
Please knock, the bell doesn't work.

### NOTICE IN HEALTH FOOD SHOP WINDOW
Closed due to illness.

### IN AN OFFICE
Would the person who took the ladder yesterday
Bring it back or further steps will be taken.

### IN ANOTHER OFFICE
After tea break, staff should empty the teapot and
Stand upside down on the draining board.

### IN A LAUNDROMAT
Automatic washing machines
Remove all your clothes when the light goes out.

### IN A LONDON DEPARTMENT STORE
Bargain Basement Upstairs.

### OUTSIDE A SECONDHAND SHOP
We exchange everything
Bicycles, washers, dryers, etc.
Bring your wife and get a wonderful bargain.

### MESSAGE ON LEAFLET
*If you cannot read, this leaflet*
*Will tell you how to get lessons.*

*GROUP LEADER ASKING:*
*Can you tell us the hour*
*And make us aware of our*
*Designated appointment time.*

# MY SUNSHINE STATE

I have lived in Florida since 1995
Love it here, would not change
Just happy being alive
But I also liked
Visiting California's Pacific Coast
San Francisco, L.A., Long Beach, San Diego
Grand exciting trip
Along highway to Monterey and Palm Springs

Enjoy viewing ships
Moored for sailing
Wishing I could exhort
Boarding everyone when they leave port
In evenings what a glorious sight
For a setting sun
Such a blessing to have simple fun.

# M/S ITALIA

The year was 1975
Oldest granddaughter's high school graduation
It was time for a special celebration.

Now nearly 35 years ago
Memories still linger
Of our cruise numbered 15/75
To the Caribbean and South America
Aboard M/S Italia
Linea "C" Costa Line.

I ponder what it would be like
To take Karen and sail the route again
On one of the new magnificent mega ships
Even take Chelsea along
Maybe Rita and Tricia could join too
I am told the accommodations are splendid
And no matter the need
Someone is always there to heed
So let's think about this again
And maybe do a cruise in 2010.

# *LIFE*

I climbed the peak of happiness
More than understanding
Realizing when I reached the top
Noticed others waited for a landing
Seeking help
Stood single file
All were waiting
Just like me for a new life worthwhile
A meeting held
Then suddenly
Passed the test
Did our best
Found life was blue skies

I will not walk again by myself
Some days must add a prayer
Answer my own question
Someone will lead me there
When the clock stops ticking
I must realize storm clouds are gone
Then sun will shine for everyone
And all returning joy
Also beautiful blue skies
From early morn
Leaving pleasure
Bring summer to fall.

# *THERE IS HOPE*

The splendor of living
In a country filled with hope
Dawn brings blessings
Why sit and mope
November 2, 2008
Brought cause to celebrate
A change in administration
May help bring elation
Time for a new beginning
An end to the war suffering
Refresh our tarnished economy
Renew diplomatic relations
With leaders of foreign nations
While seeking bipartisan cooperation.
Chase away frustration, anger and fears
Bring back smiles about our U.S. worldwide
Peace of mind, ease tribulations
We will have no cause for more tears.

# JUST BE HAPPY

Just be happy when you can
Drive away evil any way you plan
Being justified
Is your helpful guide.

Like Russell, he was a kind guy
Brother number four
A helpful one to everyone
Whether on the job or at home
His loving family was proud of him
Dorothy, Kathleen, Barbara
Gregory and Donald
Thinking of them brings a smile again
Russ made their lives worthwhile.

Thinking about a day to celebrate
Singing songs around the world
Where people congratulate
What a joyous venture visiting magic places
Happiness for smiling faces
Remembering by gone in all ages.

Being a wheel not my idea
A path of imagination
A boss may think
Then comes the culmination
Try your best
Be creatively helpful where you can
Use caution in tender situations
Don't add to one's aggravation.

# ALL SOULS DAY

Father Ryan offered the Mass
Remembering all souls gone before
Praying all saints to help bear the loss
My thoughts to family, friends
Filled my days gone by
Even caused sadness
Tears fill eyes and I cry
I have heavy load to travel
Saying the Hail Mary many times a day
To worthy be when receiving
The most holy sacred host
Make me kind to everyone I pray
Father, Son and Holy Ghost.

Manufactured By:     RR Donnelley
                     Momence, IL  USA
                     July , 2010